The Fault With Reality

Reality

New Experiments With Truth

ANIL KUMAR SINGH

ISBN 979-8-89186-830-4

Dedication

To,

My late parents, Basanti and Trilok Singh Syunry.

My siblings Neelam and Sunil, their spouses Darshan and Sunita.

My wife Vibha, son Aditya, daughter-in-law Theres and
nieces Kanchan, Saloni and Siyona.

Contents

Preface

Don't adjust your mind

In Doordarshan's infancy, tuning the TV set was an elaborate ritual. Images would still go wavy occasionally, sending viewers scurrying to the control knobs or the rooftop antenna. At times though a message would flash on the screen: 'There's a fault with transmission, don't adjust your TV set'.

Today, when information is indistinguishable from disinformation, analysis from perception management, fact from fiction, there's no one to warn us: 'There's a fault with reality, don't adjust your mind'.

So, when *The Free Press Journal*, a newspaper with roots in the freedom struggle, invited me to write a weekly column on current topics, the obvious theme and title were: The Fault With Reality. For the next two years, which coincided with the COVID-19 lockdown, I had a free run.

Friends, fellow journalists and acquaintances commented on my pieces but the sharpest reactions came on national issues, which invariably centred around the Prime Minister.

People were surprised that someone was openly critical of the PM. The mainstream media had begun crawling to the extent that joint statements by eminent citizens were buried deep inside the newspaper. The comatose Opposition was yet to think of a pushback. The Supreme Court watched as an ailing octogenarian Jesuit died in custody for 'conspiring to kill the PM'. Such were the times that several of my friends and relatives dared not acknowledge my pieces on social media although they were full of praise for them in private.

Now, I cannot say whether it was my piece that a former colleague shared on social media but one such piece about the PM almost cost him a chance to become a judge of the Bombay High Court.

My column though was in no way Modi-centric. Plain truths were told about the Supreme Court, civil servants, the Mumbai police, industrialists, architects and doctors too.

Then all of a sudden, the axe fell. On May 9, 2022, I was told to stop writing with immediate effect. It was baffling as the same newspaper had entrusted me with editorials as well. In hindsight, it seems to have been precipitated by the government's ire at the splash made by the Paris-based Reporters Without Borders' damning report on press freedom in India.

Ironically, my last column, 'India isn't a safe place for comedians either' (May 7, 2022), chastised the Indian media for its discreet silence on the stifling of dissent, instead preferring to cite a foreign agency's report.

To think that this happened in a newspaper whose founding editor Swaminathan Sadanand opted to sell his house and fields to pay a ruinous fine imposed by the British government when an apology would have sufficed: A case of sacrificing real estate for the fourth estate.

Friends consoled me: *"Column he toh bund kiya, tumko toh nahin"*, meaning I was lucky to have freedom after speech. What happened to the BBC and NewsClick proves them right.

It's a pity because The Fault With Reality was basically straight-think featuring diverse topics: Mumbai city, mental health, Urdu vs Hindi, serial killers, affluenza, architecture and even Indian love poems.

Anil Kumar Singh

December 12, 2023

Foreword

Gentle but hard-hitting

It was in the aftermath of the communal riots in then Bombay (now Mumbai), in the early 1990s, that I first met Anil Singh, Correspondent of *The Times of India*. Already familiar with the journalistic world on account of my activism in consumer issues related to telecom and also my involvement with the *Economic and Political Weekly* (EPW), I had begun to witness aberrations in journalistic commitment to balanced and objective reporting. I was, therefore, all the more apprehensive of receiving a supportive and sympathetic response from the press in a deeply communally charged Bombay at all levels of society.

I was struck by the freshness, sensitivity and positive welcome I received from Anil when I went to see him at TOI to explain the objectives of the Mohalla Committee Movement and the Cricket for Peace programme we had launched under the leadership of Julio Ribeiro, former Director-General of Police (Punjab and Gujarat) and former ambassador to Romania.

Even at that stage of his career, Anil's commitment to taking up issues of communal harmony, city development issues, environment and the agonies of ordinary citizens and to plug for solutions came through sharply, compared to those of many reporters who did not deviate from their assigned beats.

I am, therefore, not therefore surprised by the variety of issues that he has found time to reflect upon, write and even suggest practical solutions to adopt — not only by those in governance, but also by activists, to bring about the realisation of specific goals in their causes, more visibly effectively and quickly.

But Anil goes many steps further than his beat experience or the love for the city that he has spent the better part of his life. He is forthright in his pithy observations on the judiciary, bold and caustic and as it needs to be said on the civil servants who run (or ruin?) this country, critical of the deplorable failures of handling the COVID disaster and appreciative when there is a sincerity of approach in the transparent management of the same epidemic.

His column is not Modi-centric, but he has not hesitated from gently exposing the Hindutva brigade. His piece on Valentine's Day is a gentle riposte to the Bajrang Dal and shows that being liberal and romantic can go hand in hand — maybe much more in "Bharatiya sanskriti"!

Though it must be the articles, Temples of Modern India and the Mahatma of the New Millennium with its quirky humour that would have truly riled the shadowy censors of the I & B Ministry that put the final full stop to his association with *The Free Press Journal*.

Maybe it is time that a future liberal government at the Centre (fingers crossed) by law would ban the ownership of the Press by business houses and encourage the new trends in press freedom that YouTube has proliferated.

I would recommend the new generations of journalists to read through the gentle but hard-hitting writings in The Fault with Reality, to learn how to be forthright and yet be encouragingly positive in journalism.

— Achintya Mukherjee, civil rights activist

Time capsule of the pandemic years

News is the most perishable of commodities. Famously, it used to be said that today's newspaper is tomorrow's fish wrapper. Nowadays most news is consumed digitally but the metaphor remains valid: news is ephemeral.

But in another sense a newspaper is like good wine: its value goes on increasing with time. What would we not give to lay our hands on a newspaper of 16 August 1947 or 29 June 1914 (the day following the assassination of Archduke Franz Ferdinand) or any day of 1857?

And what is true of news is true of newspaper columns as well. The history books of today suggest that India rose as one in response to Gandhi's call for non-cooperation in 1920. But how did commentators of the day react? Without the lens of time to refract their observations did they realise that they were viewing a historical event? Or did its significance completely escape them? It would be interesting to know. There would be no better source than the newspaper editorials of the day.

This book consists of Anil Singh's column, The Fault With Reality, that appeared in The Free Press Journal between 2020 and 2022. It is an eclectic collection, with subjects ranging from the suicide of Sushant Singh Rajput and mental health awareness to the effect of global warming on our cities, from plastic pollution to police encounters. Anyone looking for a time capsule of 2020-22 would find it here.

As we might guess, the tone (and undertone) of the book is political. And how could it have been otherwise in a year in which the hate politics of the BJP dominated all discussions, even those ostensibly unconnected with politics? This was the period in which intellectuals opposed to the BJP were put in jail or continued to be incarcerated while gangsters made their way to Parliament, a period in which nearly every known institution of government was sought to be subverted in the cause of narrow political interests.

But when future generations look at this column they will realise that there was cause for optimism even in these dark times and that communal politics did not overwhelm everything else. Thus, there is commentary on mental health, agriculture, sport, civic amenities or the lack thereof, the problems of the elderly, and much else. Even in these areas, the opinion expressed in these columns is gloomy, but far from hopeless.

Zhou Enlai, when asked what he thought of the French Revolution, said that it was too early to tell. The story may be apocryphal but the idea was appropriate: it takes a very long time for the consequences of any event to completely play themselves out. If Anil's reading of contemporary events is right, the commentators of 20 or 50 years hence will agree with his interpretation.

— Philip George, journalist and author

Striking a blow for civil society

I remember Anil Singh as an 'active' or should I say 'activist' Chief Reporter of the Mumbai edition of *The Times of India*. He especially had his antenna out for new and breaking stories that voiced the pain of the citizen on the street.

One evening, I called him to tip him off about a huge environmental devastation being wrought by the construction of the Dighi port in Raigad district. Among illegal excavation of hills and the coastline, the excavators were also mowing down a bunch of rare baobab trees. These beautiful specimens with huge water-filled trunks, had made their way to our western seafront from East Africa in the 16th century via the Sidhi rulers.

Anil was excitement personified and immediately assigned a reporter to find out. A report in the ToI followed. Those days ToI was a powerful institution. The district collector, who had been ignoring CRZ rules and the savagery of the coastline, moved into action and clamped down on the contractors.

Anil Singh moved on from the ToI to independent writing and focused especially on travel, environment and the degeneration of the city. He did a stint with the Free Press Journal, and though he left its rolls, continued to write a plucky column calling out corruption and bad policy of the establishment. His editorials and commentary on the deteriorating housing and transport situation in Mumbai were especially noticed. Unfortunately, he was also noticed by those in government tracking media, and Anil's FPJ column was discontinued. That is the price, I suppose, writers pay for having a straight spine.

News media in India is in the throes of a crisis. Nearly 100% of television/broadcast media and about 50% of the print media have thrown in the towel and unabashedly support the Modi regime. Those who try and take a 'neutral' stance are shrinking by the day. For those like Anil, there are very few platforms on which they can report and comment. Fortunately, there is a glimmer of hope as the footprint of digital media expands. Here too it is daily hide-n-seek; but by its very nature, digital media is difficult to control. Hopefully, Anil Singh and journos like him will always have an audience.

His book as a collection of his column in the FPJ will be part of that body of journalism that left its mark on civil society. It will also flag the fact that a determined bank of writers are still willing to take on the establishment and work to bring out the Truth.

— Gurbir Singh, Chairman, Mumbai Press Club

Draws us out of our cloistered existence

Anil Singh has a beatific smile: it suggests a genial temperament, and which is so. But lurking behind the benign smile is sarcasm and an incisive mind which manifests in his writing. The sarcasm is biting, finds its mark but leaves no scars. Instead, it brings a smile to your face — almost as benign as his own.

His book, 'The Fault with Reality', is at one level an insight into our deceptively genial existence where we don't wish to look at the warts and eyesores. This outlook has lulled us into a false sense of complacency, with each one of us not wanting to stir out of our comfort zone.

Anil draws us out of our cloistered existence, he seduces us with his enticing turn of phrase to confront us with lies and half-truths that make up our world of make-believe. He mirrors our mundane and mechanical lives, tells us how, deprived of empty spaces, we have begun to almost relish our cramped lives, he reminds us that our wetlands are not our wastelands, how incorrigible we all are when it comes to cricket and politics.

He digresses every now and then, delves into affairs of heart, goads us into penning a poem to our Valentine, reminding us that romantic love is not alien to Bharatiya Sanskriti. On one hand, he craves for the ubiquitous bicycle and, on the other, about Gandhi — the lost compass.

Pick up his book while travelling by rail or air — you wouldn't like the journey to end.

— Shailender Dhawan, Editor, *The Free Press Journal*

Uncompromising

When I first met Anil Kumar Singh way back in the 1980s, he struck me as an idealistic, open-minded, yet slightly skeptical young man who wanted to learn as much as he could about the craft of journalism and its possibilities in as short a time as possible. He was an invaluable member of the team at the freshly recast Sunday Magazine of *The Free Press Journal* which I edited in Bombay (as Mumbai was known then), brimming with new ideas and open to venturing into untested waters. After a successful career in mainstream journalism, Anil is today a respected columnist, his idealism, sense of humour and questioning mind informing his writing with a freshness of perspective, boldness and vigour that is hard to come by in these troubling times when journalists are constantly looking over their shoulder, wondering when the axe will fall on them. Whether it be his concern for the environment, or his critique of the assault on democratic institutions or his lament of the lack of probity in the political arena, Anil's writing is uncompromising in its intent to lay bare the ills of present day Indian society – an intent which is at the core of good journalism anywhere in the world.

It is ironic that the axe did eventually fall on Anil's column in the 95-year-old FPJ, a newspaper that was an avid supporter of India's independence movement under the stewardship of S Sadanand, its first editor. Hopefully, this will not mean the end to his contribution to the world of journalism, a contribution that is more valuable and relevant today than it has ever been.

— Prema Viswanathan, journalist and author

Conversation starter

I have known Anil for close to four decades. His writing and the topics he chooses to write on reflect his sincere, heartfelt concerns. In this collection of his writings in *The Free Press Journal*, Anil has been focussed on issues involving the police and affairs of the local civic bodies. Although the stories involve institutions, Anil's central concerns are the human beings, the people. He seeks an insight into the human condition. In this endeavour he explores the lives, tribulations, of citizens and also the bureaucrats, the officials and the leadership that is involved in the story giving the story a humane touch.

Data, events, phenomena have human interaction, relationships at their centre and Anil is able to bring this connection to the fore effectively.

There is a specific kind of relationship between the citizen and the bureaucracy, especially since the State is an instrument of power and monopolises violence and bureaucrats do not necessarily see themselves as causing violence by their actions. It is always and anywhere an uneasy relationship. In his writings, Anil highlights this violence as it unfolds. The violence hurts people's faith and trust both with respect to the State and each other. More often than not, the citizen is shortchanged in the exchange.

The pieces published in this book are to be read and mulled over, not forgotten. These are conversation starters, but the conversations will be decidedly uncomfortable and disturbing primarily because while Anil states the problem, the solutions are complex and need working over. The first step towards those solutions is to start the conversations and this book makes a contribution in that space.

— Sanjay Ranade, author and journalism teacher

Acknowledgements

My sincere thanks to:

Shailender Dhawan, editor of *The Free Press Journal*, for trusting me as a writer.

My former editors and guiding stars, Arun Sadhu and Darryl D'Monte, who will live on through their work.

Sanjeev Dayal, former Director-General of Police, Maharashtra, for playing the contrarian.

My friends Jagdish Rattanani, Ashley D'Mello, Harish Nambiar, Philip Chacko, S Krishnadas and Krishnaraj Rao for valuable advice.

Sandeep Thakur, Nagendra Pant, Carol Andrade, Jairam Menon, Hiren Bose, Raju Bist, Shiva Thekkepat, V K N Nair, B N Kumar, Geeta Bhagat and my former colleagues at *The Times of India* for their interest and inputs.

Last but not least, to the hundreds of readers on social media for their bouquets as well as brickbats.

Section 1

PM Modi and His Methods

Mahatma of the New Millennium?

*Modi embodies the hopes and aspirations of millions today,
just as Mahatma Gandhi once did.*

Is it sacrilege to say that Indian Prime Minister Narendra Damodardas Modi is the Mahatma Gandhi of the 21st century? No one's really interested in knowing what Gandhians think of it although they will rightly point out that the title Mahatma belongs only to Mohandas Karamchand Gandhi.

Modi has captured the imagination of Indians in the same way Gandhi had done during the freedom struggle. Just as they believed that Gandhi would deliver them *'azadi'*, they now believe that Modi has curbed corruption and that he will pull them out of poverty. Both Gujaratis are seen as selfless and of course no one can accuse them of nepotism.

Like Gandhi, the PM is a great communicator. The former gave us slogans such as 'Do or die' and 'Quit India', the latter, *'Na khaunga, na khaane doonga'* and promised to end *'bhay, bhookh aur bhrashtachar'*.

Like the Mahatma, Modi understands the power of symbolism. The former spun the *'charkha'* and launched the salt satyagraha, the latter started his national campaign with *'chai pe charcha'* and provided cooking gas to rural women.

Gandhi sang *'bhajans'* and used phrases such as Ram *rajya*, Modi has delivered the Ram temple at Ayodhya. Gandhi championed *'swadeshi'*, the use of Indian goods, Modi says we must be *'atmanirbhar'*, self-reliant. The former said the lavatory must be as clean as the drawing room, the latter said, *'pehle shauchalay, phir devalay'.* Gandhi worked 16 hours a day and led an austere life, Modi claims to do that and calls himself a *fakir.*

For a significant percentage of Indians, Modi is the new messiah, whether you call him the new Mahatma or a *Mahayogi* or a *Mahanayak.*

Today, the common man is led to believe that Gandhi handed over India to a bunch of barristers, anglicized gentry – *'suit-boot ki sarkar'* — led by Nehru who thrust alien concepts such as secularism on us.

Modi, on the other hand, is a homespun hero, someone who struggled against poverty, someone who speaks their language, who is wholly Indian in spirit, who is not hesitant about flaunting his Hindu identity and is unabashedly majoritarian. He embodies their hopes and aspirations today just as Gandhi once did.

Now, one can dispute all this. Gandhi harvested hope, Modi harvests hatred. Gandhi appealed to the higher values, Modi is a rabble-rouser. The Mahatma insisted that the end should not justify the means and called off the Non-cooperation movement at its height in 1922 after the Chauri Chaura incident when a mob burnt a police station with the 22 cops and three civilians in it.

Modi's handling of the Godhra riots which saw over 1,000 deaths was not seen as *'raj dharma'* by his own party leader, Atal Bihari Vajpayee.

Gandhi was a voracious reader and corresponded with world leaders and philosophers, Modi mixes history with mythology, confuses science with obscurantist mumbo-jumbo and revels in selfies with PMs and Presidents.

Gandhi is known for his aphorisms; The earth provides enough to satisfy every man's need, but not every man's greed; The weak can never forgive. Forgiveness is the attribute of the strong; an eye for eye only ends up making the whole world blind. Modi is known for his *'jumlas'; 'Achche din aayenge',* Make in India, vocal for local, more crop per drop, *'mein bhi chaukidar'...*

The former wrote about his 'experiments with truth' and his life was an open book, the latter experiments with electoral truths or identity politics and only certain pages of his life are open to the reader. The former was able to assemble a galaxy of talent, the latter has assembled a phalanx of yes men.

Before he became the PM, Modi spoke of putting up a Gandhi museum in Gandhinagar, featuring tableaux of 365 incidents from his life but what eventually came up was the Rs 3,000-cr statue of Sardar Patel at Kevadia.

Outside India though, Modi pays lip service to Gandhi. Writing in *The New York Times* on the occasion of the Mahatma's 150th birth anniversary last year, he said, "Let us work shoulder to shoulder to make our world prosperous and free from hate, violence and suffering. That is when we will fulfil Mahatma Gandhi's dream." Wonder why he did not think of Gandhi during the Godhra riots in 2002 when he was the CM of Gujarat.

If Gandhi is being appropriated by Modi, where are the Gandhians? Why have they sequestered themselves in their 'ashrams' when they need to counter it in cyber space as well as on the street. Gandhi would surely launch a satyagraha against the undeclared Emergency of today, he would join the Shaheen Baug sit-in, side with Prashant Bhushan over the contempt of court case and demand the release of scholars such as Sudha Bharadwaj, Anand Teltumbde, Gautam Navlakha and Varavara Rao and others held for over two years in the farcical Bhima Koregaon case.

What was the Rowlatt Act against which Mahatma Gandhi launched a satyagraha in March 1919; it allowed certain political cases to be tried without juries and permitted suspects to be interred without a trial. Gandhi was even tried for sedition in 1922 and sentenced to six years imprisonment. Today, those opposing similar Acts are dubbed urban Naxals and anti-nationals and are being locked up under the draconian Unlawful Activities Prevention Act meant to curb terrorist activities.

There have been Gandhian efforts such as human rights activist Harsh Mander's *Karwan- e-mohabbat* which met the victims of mob lynchings across India. However, they do not get the kind of support from civil society or the media coverage that they deserved. What then is the use of writing scholarly pieces on the relevance of Gandhi on his birth anniversary?

The question to ask is not whether Gandhi is relevant today but whether we are relevant to Gandhi today. Gandhi stood for the universal values of truth and compassion and if we have forsaken him it shows we have lost our moral compass.

Barely 300 people visit the Gandhi museum at Mani Bhavan on October 2, half of them foreign tourists. The bungalow near Chowpatty beach in Mumbai served as Gandhiji's residence and the headquarters of the Indian National Congress from 1917 to 1934.

Gandhi learnt spinning here. The first call for mass satyagraha was given from here. The call to the nation to make public bonfires of imported cloth and to patronise '*khadi*' was given from here, as was the call to observe January 26, 1930 as Independence Day.

The same Bollywood which is being humiliated today sparked a revival of interest in Gandhi with the two *Munnabhai* films. Why do we wait for Bollywood to make Gandhi sexy? Why can't we, as Gandhi said, be the change we want to see?

The answer is that it is hard work. Good, Gandhi said, travels at a snail's pace. "Non-violence is a tree of slow growth. It grows imperceptibly but surely. And then mere goodness is not of much use", Gandhi said. "Goodness must be joined with knowledge, courage and conviction. One must cultivate the fine discriminating quality which goes with spiritual courage and character."

Coming back to the original question, one can say that Modi being called the new Mahatma will not go down well with his parent organization, the Rashtriya Swayamsevak Sangh (RSS), which is virulently anti-Gandhi. In fact, RSS circles described his assassination as Gandhi '*vadh*', a term used to describe the slaying of a demon.

Yet, the way we have forsaken Gandhi makes one feel that perhaps India was lucky to get freedom as early as it did. We also fail to appreciate the achievement of our founding fathers in defying all doomsday predictions and keeping India from disintegrating. And later to prevent it from turning into a mirror image of Pakistan.

Maybe the point to ponder is that the world knows of only two thinkers from India; Buddha and Gandhi; and we have no use for both of them.

✳ ✳ ✳

Agriculture Versus Agree-culture

The farmers need to realize the inevitability of reforms and the government that consensus can't be achieved through stealth and strong-arm tactics.

It has been two weeks since the farmers have been agitating but most urban Indians, who grasped the complexities of the US polls, can't quite comprehend why the peasants are revolting. The *kisaan andolan* truly brings out the urban-rural divide in India.

The city slicker can hold forth on TikTok versus Telegram but not *Kharif* versus *Rabi*; India's two major farming seasons. How many of us know that they are taken from the Arabic for autumn and spring respectively.

Of course, when it comes to virtual farming the townie is a seasoned hand at *FarmVille, Hay Day, Big Little Farmer…* a far cry from Mahatma Gandhi's belief: "To forget how to dig the earth and tend the soil is to forget ourselves". A *bania*, he learned this first-hand at the Tolstoy Farm in South Africa and then by fighting farmers' battles in India.

Kharif and *Rabi* also explain how hordes of farmers have deserted their fields – after all, crops can't be grown with a click — to besiege Delhi. *Kharif* crops — paddy, jowar, bajra, etc, which are sown in the monsoon — have been harvested and the winter *Rabi* crops — wheat, gram, mustard, etc, have been sown — leaving the farmer with time on his hands.

So divorced from nature are city dwellers that 'urban farming' is the latest fad. These kitchen-gardeners are so pleased with their tomatoes and chillies that Instagram is flooded with their achievements or should one say, *growth* stories.

Imagine the bemused farmer when Bollywood peaches pose with lemons and cucumbers. Actually, few city-dwellers have seen vegetables *in situ*, prior to being plucked. The biggest draw at Mumbai's annual Fruit and Flower show is not orchids but brinjals and bottle gourds.

Most of us have no idea where the food on our plate comes from. Mumbai's wheat comes from UP and Punjab, the pulses from Bihar, some vegetables from Gujarat, milk, at times, is sourced from Karnataka and fruits from all across the state and the country.

Our farmers not only feed the country but also export grains, fruits and processed food products to 120 countries. In 2016, India exported $38 billion worth of agricultural products, making it the seventh-largest agricultural exporter worldwide.

However, the average Indian farmer owns a small piece of land; less than one hectare, which is 2.5 acres or four *bighas*; slightly bigger than a football field. Given our low farm productivity, the *kisaan* grows just enough for himself.

Despite the Green Revolution quadrupling production in five decades, the national record for wheat per hectare is just 6.5 tons (Punjab) whereas the world record is 17.4 tons (New Zealand). The average wheat yield per hectare in India ranges from 1.6 tons in Madhya Pradesh to 4.2 tons in Punjab.

At the minimum support price (MSP) – the price at which the government purchases directly from the farmer — of Rs 2,000 per quintal, 1.6 tons amount to Rs 32,000 and 4.2 tons to Rs 84,000. Why would a farmer slog six months for this paltry sum when he can make more money selling peanuts at Mumbai's traffic junctions?

The average agriculture household income in 2016-'17 was a mere Rs 8,931 per month (NABARD). The rural per capita income, in terms of net-value added, is less than half the urban figure; Rs 41,000 versus Rs 98,000.

So, most tillers can't afford farmhands, who prefer the *sarkari* employment guarantee scheme (under the Mahatma Gandhi National

Rural Employment Guarantee Act), which ensures them Rs 200 a day for at least 100 days a year.

If the farmhand migrates to Mumbai, he gets Rs 700 per day as an unskilled *begari* labourer. And once he learns carpentry, masonry or plumbing, he can quote his own price. There are plumbing contractors who go from site to site in a Honda City.

Prime Minister Narendra Modi aims to double farm income through increased productivity of crops and livestock, greater efficiency of input use, increase in crop intensity, diversification towards high-value crops and improved price realization by farmers. All this takes patience, persistence and planning.

The set of three new laws Modi has brought in are part of his grand doubling scheme and they encourage large-scale farming. Farmers say that the laws were passed hurriedly without consulting them. They are also afraid of a corporate takeover of agriculture.

Anyway, after the disastrous demonetization and the GST mess, the PM needs more than just *jumlas,* such as 'More crop per drop', to be taken seriously.

On the other side, having been treated with disdain and having been called names, the infuriated farmers have hardened their stance even though the government is willing to bend. As Confucius noted: "A general of a large army may be defeated, but you cannot defeat the determined mind of a peasant".

A slight digression here to 2011 in Deesa, 60 km north of Ahmedabad, when Modi was the CM of Gujarat. After three bumper crops, cold storages ran out of space for the prized potatoes of Deesa. Prices fell to Rs 3/kg which did meet even transport costs. Distressed farmers started dumping sacks by the river.

After months of petitioning Modi, farmers staged a spectacular protest; dumping truckloads of the tuber on the main street to be crushed by passing vehicles which soon started skidding on the squishy mess. The sub-divisional magistrate was greeted with a hail of potatoes. Cops got the same 'ouch potato' treatment.

We may poke fun at the ignorance of the urban elite on matters agricultural but there exist win-win urban-rural tie-ups. For example, Crop-Connect, set up by two young city-bred entrepreneurs, helps cultivators meet niche market demands, such as linking remote kiwi farms in the Northeast with metro markets. Another of their initiatives is assembling a package for diabetics by sourcing a rice variety from Karnataka, a millet variety from Uttarakhand and jamun powder made by tribals in Jharkhand.

Can't there be a similar win-win solution to the current impasse? Most certainly, there can. And India needs it desperately.

The farmers need to realize the inevitability of reforms and the government that everything can't be achieved through stealth and strong-arm tactics. The ruling party needs to build a consensus on farm reforms. Debate it. Agriculture is not agree-culture.

As the agitation snowballed, it has dawned on the decision-makers that they too could have behaved like the ignorant and arrogant urbanite. The government is willing to tweak the new laws that do away with MSP and that would have left farmers to the vagaries of the market.

It now needs to convince the farmers that allowing the sale and purchase of crops outside the state government-regulated market yards, the *mandis* of the APMC (agricultural produce market committee), will not harm their interests. That the Bihar fiasco will not be repeated. If need be, safeguards can be built into the law.

Instead of battling farmers, the government should be fighting the farmers' battles. That will lead to Ram *rajya*.

Modi's Temples of Modern India

Denigrating Nehru on WhatsApp is easy but upstaging him as a PM is a challenge.

Modi is no Nehru fan and now he has demonstrated that he differs from the latter's definition of temples of modern India. The PM was not at Kakrapar, Gujarat, this July 22 to celebrate the reaching a scientific milestone by the nuclear power plant there but he will be at Ayodhya on August 5 to lay the foundation stone for the Ram temple.

Denigrating Nehru on WhatsApp is easy but upstaging him as a PM is a challenge. If Modi is up to it, he can start by rectifying the first PM's mistakes.

Nehru built big dams, heavy industries, institutes of scholastic and scientific excellence, etc as the temples of modern India but his record in public health and primary education is nothing to talk about. The man was a visionary but an elitist approach prevented the gains from percolating to the poor. This explains why India ranks 129th out of 189 nations in the human development index despite all the scientific and industrial progress.

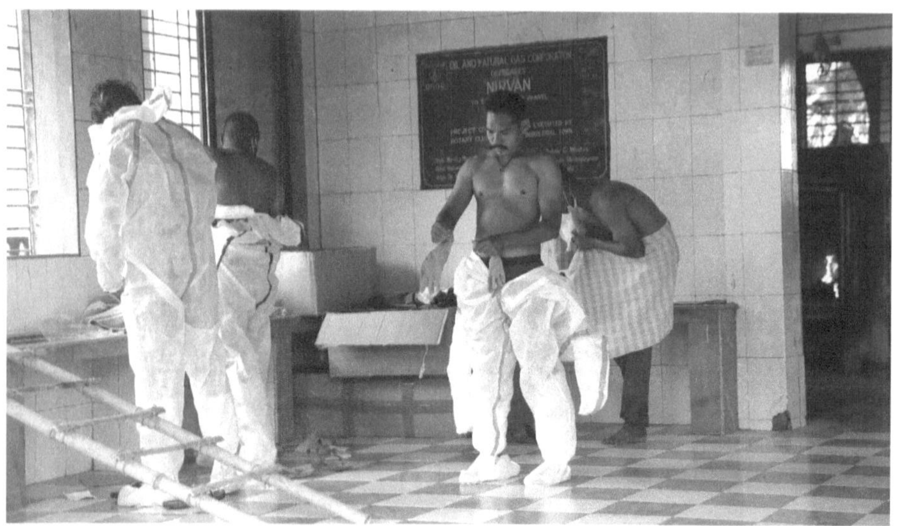

The pandemic was the perfect opportunity to revamp the public health system.
Credit: Sudharak Olwe

Modi can begin with investing more than just the measly one per cent of the GDP that the Congress-era governments did on public health. With COVID-19, he has a historic opportunity. For starters, he can replicate the AIIMS, a Nehruvian temple, in every city and rename it the Atal/ Advani Institute of Medical Sciences. After all, it is hospitals and not holy places that matter in a pandemic. Showering money rather than petals is the way to go about improving the public health infrastructure, as Kerala has shown.

Likewise, Nehru started the IITs but his report card on school education, in the words of Nobel laureate Amartya Sen, is, "lamentable". Even today primary education is so low-priority and riddled with corruption that the food at the mid-day meal scheme designed to lure poor children to schools is often unfit for human consumption.

Modi can increase the expenditure on education which is three per cent of the GDP. Instead, he is busy dismantling the JNU and the UGC, diluting the IITs and replacing academics of repute with '*bhakts*'. Matters have reached such farcical limits that ministers who can't show their own degree certificates are questioning the credentials of renowned scholars. And who can forget the HRD ministry's 'institutes of eminence' tag that included the Jio Institute which is still a proposal.

It would seem as if Modi and his masters in the RSS are in a hurry to raze the Nehruvian temples and build their own on the ruins.

As for scientific temper, some mad cow disease has afflicted our research institutes. IIT-Delhi received several proposals from top research institutions to explore the benefits of *panchagavya*, a mixture of five cow products: urine, dung, milk, ghee and curd. Some members of an alumni association of the prestigious Indian Institute of Science, Bangalore, would have gotten away with a workshop on astrology at the institute had it not been for a public outcry.

What can one say when the Union Minister for Science & Technology claims at a session of the Indian Science Congress that Stephen Hawking said that our Vedas might have a theory which is superior to Einstein's theory of E=mc^2. The peddling of such arrant nonsense and pseudoscience is what led to a nation-wide protest by scientists against "the propagation of unscientific and obscurantist ideas".

Initially, the PM too claimed that cosmetic surgery to reproductive genetics to stem cell therapy were practiced in ancient India but now he talks of promoting a scientific temper. It will be seen as lip service unless he puts his money where his mouth is and increases India's spending on science and technology, a paltry 0.8 per cent of the GDP.

Modi's own temples show his penchant for the grandiose: the economically unviable Ahmedabad-Mumbai bullet train, the environmentally unsound Char Dham highway project which has been called a Himalayan blunder, the impossible Garland canal project when the emphasis should be on potable water for all, the sluggish Namami Gange river rejuvenation project, the Sardar Patel statue and the Smart City project in metros where the act of breathing itself is equivalent to smoking 20 cigarettes a day, where civic authorities are unable to find space for a garbage dump, where sewer workers routinely choke to death.

If Narendra Modi really wants to compete with Jawaharlal Nehru he would do better not to opt for pompous projects and focus on the basics rather than the optics.

The Nation Wants to Know

Indians still believe that Narendra Modi is the best bet but wish he would stop fudging his report card.

When the PM addresses the nation from the Red Fort on our 74th Independence Day, citizens expect some plain-speak from him. Ram delivered, it's time for 'rozgaar'. Ration not 'bhashan', hope not hype, healing not hatred.

Indians still believe that Narendra Modi is the best bet as PM but they are tired of him fudging his report card. They don't want a five trillion-dollar economy, they don't want the Rs 1.70 lakh crore Corona relief package, they don't want his *Atmanirbhar* spiel, Indians just want the PM to take baby steps on the road to economic recovery.

Forget *Make in India, Skill India, Start-Up India, Stand Up India…,* Modi needs to emulate Deng Xiaoping who famously said that he did not care about the colour of the cat as long as it caught mice.

People don't want the promised Rs 15 lakh in their bank accounts, they just want banks to recover swindled public money from all the crony capitalists. They don't want pious statements on Ram *rajya,* they just want the government to come clean on electoral funding. Why is it, voters want to know, that they have to account for each paisa they have while political parties don't. After all, this is the Gangotri of corruption.

We rang bells for health staff and showered petals on hospitals but why are the salaries of doctors and nurses combatting Covid being held up? Why are citizens already without income for four months being given a shocker of an electricity bill? There is such a huge gap between promise and performance that no amount of *'jumlas'*, jingoism or jugglery can patch it up. As Lincoln said, "You can fool all the people some of the time, and some of the people all the time, but you cannot fool all the people all the time."

The problem arises from the PM's proclivity for the grandiloquent and his preoccupation with his role as the sole vote-catcher of his party. It's time Modi realized that people want to see him as their *'Pradhan Sevak'*, not as the *'pracharak'* of a political party. A Congress-*'mukt'* Bharat may be his priority but the people want him to fulfill his promise of a Bharat *'mukt'* of *'bhay, bhookh aur bhrastachar'*.

It is just as well that there are hardly any dignitaries at I-Day this time, let alone foreign dignitaries. The foreign policy of India seems to be little other than a series of selfies with world leaders. If our foreign policy was that good, why did we not see the writing on the wall when Chinese Premier Xi Jinping came visiting? Why did we lump it when our *'jigri dost'* President Trump publicly threatened India over hydroxychloroquine? Why have we alienated all our neighbours?

Coming back to bread-and-butter issues, the nation is on the brink of an economic implosion. How many shocks can it survive; demonetization, GST, COVID, civil strife, war threat? Even Lord Ram cannot save a team that scores so many self-goals.

Even Indian capitalists, who traditionally keep their traps shut, are beginning to say that Modi has 'flattened the wrong curve'; that of economy instead of Covid. As for an ignoramus like me, I only want to know why global capital deserting China prefers Vietnam over India. Has it anything to do with us managing our monetary policy like Mohammed bin Tughlak?

As for the voice of the *'aam admi'*, it has been cynically suppressed by a pliant media. Such is the headline management skill of this government that an actor's suicide dominates the front page at a time when dissidents are being labelled as urban Naxals, academicians have been either liquidated or silenced by the fear of lynch mobs and journalists and outspoken critics are being booked for sedition. Today, the indices of civil liberties in the country resemble that of Pakistan. What is this if not an undeclared Emergency?

All this does not perturb the judiciary. In fact, it restricted the freedom of speech by hauling up a senior activist lawyer for contempt of court over his Tweets. This is the same judiciary that operates through sealed covers, which takes the government at face value on preventive detention even when there is incontrovertible evidence to the contrary, which is blind to the sufferings of millions of men, women and children walking thousands of kilometres to their villages. Is this justice prevailing or justices prevailing?

It seems there is no such concept as contempt of citizens, that the 'aam admi' only wants to know how the PM prefers to eat 'aam'; how much can you suck up to the emperor-without-clothes.

How will our Prime Minister know the *janata ke mann ki baat* if he reverts to 'maun ki baat' when it comes to fielding questions from the media? Is this the same man who swears by Lord Ram who went to the extent of banishing his wife based on hearsay? How will the *Pradhan Sevak* empower the public to fight corruption if he throttles the Right to Information Act?

In fact, COVID has presented a perfect opportunity to the ruling dispensation to bypass a lot of democratic conventions. Talking of the pandemic, why is the PM silent on it now, why has he pushed the onus on to the states? He is the same man who gave 1.4 billion people just four hours before a national lockdown, something which even dictators like Idi Amin would have thought twice about.

And we have not even touched on the forbidden word, 'azadi'. The present dispensation ought to be humbled by the fact that they had no role to play in the Independence struggle, in fact they were stooges of the British.

This I-Day, we want the PM to allay the fears raised by Mahua Moitra of the Trinamool Congress about the seven early signs of Fascism evident in India: Nationalism searing into national fabric, disdain for human rights in government, subjugation and control of mass media, obsession with national security, religion and government intertwined in the country, disdain for intellectuals and the arts and erosion of independence in the electoral system.

When will the PM realize that his party has been voted to power to solve 'roti, *kapda, makaan*' issues, not to push the agenda of an outfit that believes in its own warped definition of nationalism. Modi is a mesmerizing speaker but mass hypnosis doesn't work on an audience with empty stomachs.

✳ ✳ ✳

Just *Jumlas* for the Middle Class

The skilful orator that he is, Modi transferred the onus of reviving the economy onto the citizen.

The middle class has never really featured in PM Narendra Modi's plans; the latest evidence of this is in his Independence Day speech which went on for a record 90 minutes, of which just three minutes were devoted to the middle class.

The PM listed cheap internet, the information highway and affordable smartphones as the 'ease of living' factors for the middle class. While it is true that mobile data in India is many times cheaper than elsewhere, it is because operators fought for new customers and this transient phase will end with the winner, evidently a crony capitalist, hiking charges. ('*Inka labh Zindabad!*' social commentator Aakar Patel tweeted in brilliant sarcasm.)

As for service, one only has to ask those who have MTNL broadband connections; *Mera Telephone Nahin Lagta* remains a bitter reality for them.

The PM also mentioned cheap flight tickets and the UDAN scheme for regional connectivity as a boon for the middle class. Again, cheap flight tickets are the result of competition between airlines, which also use dynamic pricing, resulting in a Delhi-Patna one-way ticket costing as much as Rs 25,000.

The well-intentioned *Udega Desh ka Aam Nagrik* or UDAN scheme enables people to fly to smaller airports but it has not taken off as expected.

The lack of a proper ecosystem for smaller players meant that the operational costs went so high that the government subsidy failed to compensate for the losses, resulting in the closure of many routes.

Falling home loan rates were harped upon, which again has more to do with the market than with a government mechanism. The PM also mentioned the special fund of Rs 25,000 cr in the last budget to complete stalled housing projects. It was to target 4.58 lakh residential units pending in 1,600 housing projects but the PM gave no update on how many houses had been delivered. However, the Real Estate Regulation Act or RERA, which the PM forgot to mention, is a welcome legislation although it has been diluted by the grant of several exemptions.

Another benefit for the middle class the PM touted was the reduced rates of GST and income tax. In the first place, the government had made a mess of GST by hastily implementing it. And the marginal reduction in income tax for the salaried was just a sleight of hand. It is insulting no doubt but why should anyone bother about the middle class when less than 10 per cent of voters pay income tax.

The PM cited the inclusion of urban co-operative banks and multi-state cooperative banks under the ambit of RBI as a guarantee for the safety of the money of middle-class families. The fact is that urban cooperative banks were already under the supervisory control of the RBI and that did not prevent some of them from going bust.

Businessmen, entrepreneurs and small farmers, the PM said, would benefit from the reforms in the MSME (micro, small and medium enterprises) and agriculture sectors. The reforms were long overdue and it will be some time before their effects are felt. What these people need is a life jacket to keep them afloat.

Now, what are the issues of the middle class? Affordable housing, health, education, quality of life... but as of now, there is only one issue, saving their jobs. The PM did not even acknowledge their pain although it is his demonetisation, GST and inept handling of the COVID lockdown that has brought them to the brink of bankruptcy. Just demonetisation shaved off two percentage points from the GDP growth rate; every one per cent growth in GDP takes two million Indians out of poverty.

But who cares about all this when the priority is to topple non-BJP governments by hook or by crook. In any case, the *'bhakts'* maintain that India is going through short-term pain because Modi is trying to clean the mess created by the Congress in the last 60 years. They believe that it is because of Modi that the Indian economy has not gone the way of Venezuela and Brazil.

Instead of softening the blow for it, the middle class is being hit with humongous bills; in Maharashtra it is the electricity bills. The state's minister for power even offered to provide loans to consumers to pay their electricity bills when he should have been questioning the bills. No wonder jesters say that the GDP is increasing; prices of Gas, Diesel and Power!

The middle class, especially pensioners, rely on their savings and fixed deposits but interest rates have hit rock bottom. And there's nothing by way of social security for the Indian middle class, which has no parallel anywhere in the world as a skilled but vastly exploited workforce.

Where in the world, except in metros like Mumbai, do you see ten people dying each day in the effort to reach their workplaces, either falling off crowded local trains or being run over by trucks and buses after falling into potholes. The proletariat can only pray to Lord Ram for divine intervention.

Economists are already talking of permanent damage to the Indian economy. The self-congratulatory tone and tenor of the PM's speech though suggests that we are in the middle of Ram *rajya*, not recession. It is pertinent here to ask why the PM is so optimistic when the Centre has not even paid the states their share of the GST.

The skilful orator that he is, Modi transferred the onus of reviving the economy on to the citizens. He peppered his speech with praise for the middle class and for the people of India who have 'risen to every occasion.'

Sample this: "The strength and energy of the common Indian is the foundation of the *Atmanirbhar Bharat Abhiyan*. Relentless work is going on at every level to maintain this strength." It resonates with the Emergency-era slogan, 'There is no substitute for hard work'. What is this if not a social version of the truism of the Indian economy that 'profits are privatised and losses are nationalised'.

Nowhere is the hypocrisy more evident than in taxation. Corporate income tax was reduced after a shrill media campaign; yes, money speaks, even when the media is gagged; but the tax hounds have been let loose on small-scale industrialists, entrepreneurs and the middle class.

Stiff targets have been set for I-T officials. Tax terror, which Modi promised to end as opposition leader, is back. Draconian steps are being taken with strange demand notices with retrospective effect... Even Modi fan Mohandas Pai, former chief financial officer of Infosys, was provoked to say that his firm had "filed returns in over 30 countries but no country treats taxpayers as badly as India does."

Forget Modi and Pai, look at the look at the role of the middle class and the working class in the freedom struggle, in fighting the Emergency, in opposing the ongoing undeclared Emergency despite the risk of being locked up for years without trial under charges of sedition or anti-national activities and last but not the least, in the fight against the deadly COVID pandemic.

Perhaps the closest the PM came to the truth in his I-Day speech was when he admitted that professionals from the middle class had made a name for themselves in the world today. "Whatever opportunities that the middle class gets, they make the most out of it and therefore the middle class needs freedom from government interference."

Modi said that the middle class wants to do away with governmental intrusion and red tape. To quote him verbatim: "They want opportunities and an open playing field. Our government is working towards helping the middle class achieve their dreams. The middle class can make miracles happen."

The politicians may just intone it but Mr Prime Minister the Indian masses are saying it from their hearts and through their deeds, 'Vande mataram!'

✳ ✳ ✳

Stop Playing Politics Over Population

Our focus should be on the profound economic and social impacts of slowing population growth.

The just-released fifth National Family Health Survey (NFHS) which reveals that India's population is stabilising robs the BJP of a potent poll issue. It can no longer raise the bogey of population explosion and target one community for it. Neither can it spread the canard that Hindus would be outnumbered by Muslims.

Yet, Prime Minister Modi harped on it as recently as August 15, 2019, although he was careful not to name any community. "Population explosion will cause many problems for our future generations," he said, going on to equate having small families with patriotism.

"There is a vigilant section of citizens which stops to think before bringing a child into the world, whether they can provide for him/her, they don't leave it to fate or to the community. Those who follow the policy of small family also contribute to the development of the nation, it is also a form of patriotism."

Politicians across the world manipulate voters with the fear of rapid population growth in a neighbouring country/continent or in specific communities within the country. Former US President Donald Trump sold the fear that a low American population would ultimately lead to a takeover by immigrants. Migration also became a crucial issue of public debate on Brexit.

It is difficult to believe that our PM was misinformed. Indian women in the 1950s averaged six births each, the Total Fertility Rate (TFR) fell to 2.7 in 2005, then to 2.2 in 2015 and now it is down to 2. India's TFR has dropped below what is deemed the replacement level. An average of less than 2.1 children per woman indicates that a generation is not producing enough children to replace itself. In other words, the survey shows that India has taken the first step towards an outright reduction in population.

The PM was perhaps pandering to the prejudices of the Rashtriya Swayamsevak Sangh (RSS), a Hindu nationalist organisation that is the progenitor of the BJP. In July 2019, Rakesh Sinha, a nominated Rajya Sabha member, who famously claimed on national TV that the Taj Mahal is a Hindu monument, tabled the Population Regulation Bill as a private member bill prescribing penalties for people for having more than two children.

Before this, Delhi BJP leader Ashwini Kumar Upadhyay had filed a public interest petition in the Delhi High Court demanding stringent legislation to control the population. In 2015, then Gorakhpur MP Yogi Adityanath conducted an online poll asking if the Modi government should formulate a policy to control population. Since Independence, 35 such bills have been tabled by MPs from various parties, including 15 from the Congress, which paid dearly for 'nasbandi', its forced sterilisation programme during the Emergency.

Prompted by the PM's utterances on population explosion, the BJP-led Assam government had immediately implemented the two-child norm, barring those having more than two offspring from state government jobs. Eight states, including non-BJP ones such as Maharashtra and Rajasthan, have similar provisions which include debarring people from contesting elections to Panchayati Raj institutions. In August, Uttar Pradesh moved towards a two-child policy. Four states; Chhattisgarh, Himachal Pradesh, Madhya Pradesh and Haryana; have revoked the two-child norm.

It is dawning on us that development is the best contraceptive; providing women greater access to education, health and birth control measures has a bigger impact on reducing fertility than punitive measures. For instance, Maharashtra has a TFR of 1.7 and Kerala, Punjab and West Bengal have 1.6 TFR, while Bihar and Uttar Pradesh have 3 and 2.4 TFR respectively.

Countrywide, women with no schooling have an average 3.1 children, compared to 1.7 children for women with 12 or more years of schooling.

Urbanisation is also an important reason for the decline. By 2030, as much as 41% of Indians will be living in towns and cities. In the countryside, an additional family member is a helping hand but in cities raising a child is expensive. Also in cities, women have less social pressure to have more children. The survey shows the fertility rate at 1.6% in urban areas and 2.1% in rural India.

However, the bad news is that the prevalence of anaemia has risen across age groups. As many as 57% of women aged 15-49 were anaemic in 2019-21, compared to 53% in 2015-16, while the same for men rose from 22.7% to 25%. The most formidable increase — 8.5 percentage points — was observed for children aged 6-59 months (67.1%).

No wonder the average height of Indians is falling. According to the NFHS, men have grown shorter by 1.10 cm while women by 0.12 cm. What can one expect in a country where the health budget is a measly 1.1% of the GDP?

Coming back to Muslims and population, census figures don't support the contention that they are baby breeders. According to Census 2011, the growth rate of the Muslim population witnessed a 5.3% drop compared to the previous decade whereas the growth rate of the Hindu population fell by 3.2% in the same period. The fact is that religion has little to do with fertility levels; Islamic Bangladesh has a TFR of 2.01. Even within India, the fertility rate among Muslims in Kerala is lower than the fertility rate among Hindus in Bihar.

The current moderate to slightly high fertility in a few categories of the population is because of lower education, higher infant mortality, preference for sons and lack of access to good quality family-planning services.

Another reason why Modi's alarmism is surprising is that it comes at a time when even China has opted for an overhaul of its earlier one-child policy. In 2013, China relaxed its infamous one-child policy imposed in 1979. The policy resulted in undesirable consequences such as sex-selective abortions, depressed fertility levels, irreversible population ageing, labour shortages and economic slowdown.

Also, the BJP needs to praise Nehru this time; in 1951, India was the first developing country to start a family planning programme.

It's time to stop playing politics over population and focus on the profound economic and social impacts of slowing population growth. India has entered a demographic sweet spot that will continue for another three decades; half of India's population is under 29 years of age. To encash this demographic dividend, we need to train and employ this mass of youngsters, not mess with their minds. The time for *'Sabka saath, sabka vikas, sabka vishwas'* is now.

***

Section 2

The New India

The Dismantling of Institutions

Erosion of the credibility of institutions that are the sentinels of democracy is the death knell for the republic.

The petulant prefect complains to the principal after being pulled up by the class teacher for playing favourites but is firmly put down. This analogy for the Election Commission of India (ECI) petitioning the Supreme Court (SC) after receiving a tongue-lashing from the Madras High Court for allowing political parties to violate COVID protocols captures the decline of our institutions.

It is unimaginable that the ECI would have tolerated such a flagrant violation during the regime of T N Seshan who initiated strict enforcement of the model code of conduct, voter IDs, limit on candidates' expenditure and appointing election officials from states other than the one going to polls. So doggedly and so fiercely did he implement the rules in his term as Chief Election Commissioner from '90 to '96 that he came to be known as 'Al-seshan'.

It is also surprising that high courts, which are now taking *suo motu* notice of COVID-related issues, took so long to read the writing on the wall. To be fair, the oral observations of the Madras HC that the ECI 'should be put up on murder charges probably' were a bit too harsh.

However, the ECI's ludicrous prayer to the SC that the media be restrained from reporting such remarks during hearings robbed it of whatever dignity it had. As it is, the ECI, the supposed guardian of India's democracy, is being blamed — not without any justification — for being an extension of the ruling party.

And it is not only during the recent polls in West Bengal which it spread over a record eight phases, ostensibly to give the BJP enough time to whip up a frenzy. In 2017, the ECI came under a cloud for its decision to delay the announcement of the Gujarat assembly polls schedule, supposedly to allow the PM and his party to continue distributing largesse in the state.

Another blot in its copybook was the ECI's hurried and unseemly disqualification of 20 Aam Aadmi Party MLAs from Delhi on the 'office of profit' charges, which was rejected by the SC. In fact, the apex court castigated the ECI for not examining the issue thoroughly. This is the same Constitutional body that once was referred to by the SC as one of the 'integrity institutions'.

However, the ECI and the judiciary are not the only institutions in decline. The list of bodies whose autonomy is under threat includes the RBI, the CBI, the NITI Aayog, the Chief Vigilance Commissioner (CVC), the Comptroller and Accountant General (CAG), the Chief Information Commissioner (CIC), the bureaucracy, the media and the Parliament itself.

These are the very sentinels of democracy and the erosion of their credibility is the death knell of the republic. In the words of American economist and Nobel laureate Douglass North: Institutions are 'the rules of the game in a society'.

So when the RBI was not consulted before demonetization in 2016, economic activity went down by a whopping three percentage points. Not that any lessons were learnt. The RBI's role as regulator of the banking sector has been questioned and its reserves siphoned, reducing it into an institution which presides over a limited space of monetary policy, that is, inflation targeting.

In fact, RBI deputy governor Viral Acharya has warned that governments that don't respect central bank independence "will sooner or later incur the wrath of financial markets, ignite economic fire, and come to rue the day they undermined an important regulatory institution."

Take the Central Vigilance Commission (CVC), meant to look into governmental corruption. It hit the headlines in 2018 for its dubious role in 'sorting out' the ugly fight between the CBI boss and his deputy; the same CBI which was denounced as a 'caged parrot' by the SC.

This CVC first came to notice for the right reasons in 2000 under N Vittal when it posted the names of 85 IAS and 22 IPS officers against whom it had sought criminal/departmental proceedings for major penalties since 1990.

By disbanding the erstwhile Planning Commission and replacing it with the National Institution for Transforming India (NITI) Aayog, the government lost the space for mid-term appraisals of its plans and policies. Course correction and taking stock of the economy have now become routine exercises, with uncritical acceptance due to a lack of well-researched documents. Its CEO Amitabh Kant had famously said that 'tough reforms are very difficult in the Indian context as we are too much of a democracy'.

The Chief Information Commissioner is a toothless tiger after the RTI Rules-2019, a straightforward effort to throttle one of the best transparency laws promulgated by Parliament. "The Right to Information is now threatened by judicial decisions and interpretations which are not in consonance with the law and which would weaken it," says former Central Information Commissioner Shailesh Gandhi, a recipient of the Nani Palkhivala Civil Liberties award.

The Lokpal and the Lokayuktas are ombudsmen representing the public interest in the Republic of India but how often does one hear about them.

The mess in the health system and the mishandling of the pandemic are in no small way related to the collapse of institutions. The Indian Medical Association (IMA) expressed shock and dismay recently at what it called a "blatant lie of WHO certification" for Patanjali's Coronil tablet.

To be fair to Modi though, the dismantling of institutions started with Indira Gandhi. Ever since there has been a steady erosion of trust in institutions that were supposed to balance the claims of competing interest groups while framing policies.

Economists blame the government's inability to build strong institutions as the key constraint to rapid growth. The stubborn refusal of the political class to fix key institutions and their plummeting credibility has paved the way for judicial interventions even on issues that are the traditional preserve of the political executive.

It was the failure to allocate natural wealth such as mining rights or telecom spectrum in a transparent manner that led to intervention by the courts and precipitated policy paralysis. As the links between key bureaucrats and crony capitalists emerged, even legitimate business activities came under a cloud and slowed investments.

Intellectuals keep warning that institutions provide the framework for individuals and systems to function, that their breakdown leads to a breakdown of societal functioning. The scum rises to the top and clogs institutions. The bad drives out the good. This is what Maharashtra is realizing in the Assistant Police Inspector Sachin Vaze case. These things can't be passed off as system failure, as former PM Manmohan Singh described the Harshad Mehta scam of 1992.

Honest officials survive in strong institutions that are difficult to manipulate. Weak institutions breed rogue behavior, as with former Mumbai police chief Parambir Singh, and the collective interest suffers. This is hardly the 'minimum government and maximum governance' envisaged by the PM.

Fear, Deception and Intimidation

India is going through an Orwellian nightmare.

India has been famously described as a land where many centuries co-exist but now it is also one where many versions of the truth co-exist; somewhat like the six blind men discovering an elephant.

So it is that Union health minister Harsh Vardhan claims that there is no shortage of oxygen in hospitals, so it is that Chief Minister Yogi Adityanath threatens to seize the property of anyone who conspires to defame the UP government over COVID deaths, so it is that the Indian government terms as 'completely baseless, slanderous and malicious' a report in 'The Australian' blaming Modi for leading India into a viral apocalypse.

Truly, India cuts a sorry figure in the run-up to the World Press Freedom Day on May 3, which acts as a reminder to governments of the need to respect their commitment to press freedom. UNESCO promotes it as a day of support for the media 'which are targets for the restraint, or abolition, of press freedom'. It is also a day of remembrance for journalists who have lost their lives in the pursuit of a story.

A horror story is the case of Siddique Kappan, a part-time reporter for a news portal. A native of Kerala, he was arrested by UP police in October last year when he went to Hathras in UP to report on the rape and murder of a Dalit girl. Kappan was booked for 'trying to create communal unrest in UP' and later charged under the draconian Unlawful Activities Prevention Act (UAPA), for his alleged association with the Popular Front of India, an extremist Islamist outfit. Kappan (42), who has cardiac issues, contracted COVID in prison and was shifted to a hospital in Mathura, UP, where he was chained like an animal to a hospital bed.

Hearing a habeas corpus petition filed by the Kerala Union of Working Journalists (KUWJ) on Wednesday, the Supreme Court ordered Kappan to be shifted to a hospital in Delhi for treatment. Solicitor-General Tushar Mehta, appearing for the UP government, called the KUWJ, of which Kappan is the Delhi secretary, a "purported organization of journalists which is not mainstream" whereas it has members from all mainstream and established newspapers.

Kappan's case is not unique. According to Geeta Seshu, co-editor of the Free Speech Collective, there has been a sharp rise in criminal cases lodged against journalists in India for their work, with a majority of cases in BJP-ruled states. Her research shows that in the last decade, 154 journalists in India were arrested, detained, interrogated or served show-cause notices for their professional work and a little over 40 per cent of these instances were in 2020. Nine foreign journalists faced deportation, arrest, interrogations or were denied entry into India in the last decade.

Others booked in recent years under the draconian UAPA and left to rot in jail include civil rights activists, lawyers and academicians in the 2018 Bhima Koregaon-Elgar Parishad case, students arrested in anti-CAA protests, human rights defenders, RTI activists and even an 83-year-old Jesuit priest, Stan Swamy.

A 1967 law, the UAPA has been repeatedly amended to include stringent provisions in the name of fighting terrorism. Further, a 2019 Supreme Court ruling has made it near impossible for the accused in such cases to get bail, shifting the onus of disproving charges on them. According to the National Crime Records Bureau, 1,948 people were arrested in 2019 under the UAPA, up from 999 in 2016, while convictions have been very low; in 2019, 34 persons were convicted, 16 discharged, and 92 acquitted.

The hostility against anti-establishment journalists in India — called 'presstitutes' by a Union minister and *'bikau patrakar'* (sold-out journalists) by the PM — is such that six of them, including big names such as Rajdeep Sardesai and Mrinal Pande, were booked for sedition just because they "shared misinformed news and instigated violence on Republic Day" through their tweets about the death of a farmer in police firing, which were subsequently corrected as the farmer died in a tractor crash. Also booked for the same offence was Congress MP Shashi Tharoor.

Pertinently, the six journalists and Tharoor were booked for sedition based on a single complaint by 'social worker' Arpit Mishra of Noida. And identical FIRs were filed against them in five different states.

The Congress made a point when it countered the PM's jibe about FDI being Foreign Destructive Ideology (in reference to Greta Thunberg's support to the Indian farmers' agitation) when it said that the FDI that is likely to come is Fear, Deception and Intimidation.

India is going through an Orwellian nightmare. Let alone journalists, last year, the Delhi police tried to ensnare IAS officer-turned-communal harmony activist Harsh Mander and Prof Apoorvanand of Delhi University under the UAPA when the duo criticized their lopsided handling of the Delhi riots.

Such is the bigots' hatred for independent journalists that on February 11 this year, a little-known YouTube channel posted a video calling for five of them to "be hanged". It is to be noted here that the 2017 murder of journalist Gauri Lankesh, an outspoken critic of Hindutva, is unsolved, as are the murders of rationalist Narayan Dabholkar, left-wing politician and author Govind Pansare and scholar M M Kalburgi, all of whom were for a secular India.

Is it any surprise then that India has fallen from a global ranking of 27 in 2015 to a ranking of 53 in 2020 in the Democracy Index compiled by the influential magazine, *The Economist*.

There is enormous pressure on the mainstream media to toe the government line. A day before announcing a national lockdown on March 24 last year, the PM had personally asked the owners and editors of the 20 biggest mainstream print media outlets to publish "positive stories" about the crisis and to "act as a link between government and people."

Six days later on March 31, the Union government even asked the SC to "direct" the media to publish nothing about the pandemic without confirming it with the government. Given the outcry over this unconstitutional move, the SC did not acquiesce.

Recently however, the government managed to get Twitter to censor tweets critical of India's handling of the pandemic.

To be safe, a significant part of India's mainstream media is playing a "both-sides game" to appear objective. Most are in self-censorship mode. Some newspapers and TV channels are simply dropping columnists or anchors seen as critical of the government. This is a far cry from the pre-Independence days when Swaminathan Sadanand, founder editor of *The Free Press Journal*, sold his land and his house to pay a ruinous fine instead of taking up the British offer to apologise and be pardoned.

However, there are still those who do the right thing. When the *Hindustan Times* declined to publish a piece by historian Ramchandra Guha on the Central Vista, a pet project of the PM, he announced that he was withdrawing his fortnightly column in the paper.

The mainstream media has not given up the fight. Twenty journalists covering health issues addressed ten key questions to the government on March 30 last year about its handling of the crisis and the lockdown, especially on the suppression of the fact that the pandemic had gone into community transmission.

This brings us to this year's World Press Freedom Day theme which is "Information as a public good". It serves as a call to affirm the importance of cherishing information as a public good and exploring what can be done in the production, distribution and reception of content to strengthen journalism.

Of late, the *'jugalbandi'* between the media and the judiciary has ensured that the spotlight stays on the fight against COVID. The media brought the emergency to the court's notice. Now, the courts need to see the other elephant in the room – media freedom.

As noted lawyer Fali Nariman told a gathering at the Press Club of India in New Delhi last June: "Freedom after speech – that is really what freedom of speech is all about".

* * *

Will a Ram *Mandir* Lead to Ram *Rajya?*

Donations are being solicited for a temple in the middle of a pandemic when these shrines offer no succour.

If you thought that the contentious Ram temple ceased to be an issue with the Supreme Court judgment, you were mistaken. It has now come literally to your doorstep.

Since last month, BJP workers have been going from house to house seeking donations for the construction of the Ram temple in Ayodhya.

Now, there is nothing illegal about raising funds for a religious structure as long as the trust is registered, receipts are given and accounts submitted. Donating to a cause is also an individual choice. However, the manner in which the whole thing is being carried out is disquieting.

To begin with, the Ram Janam Bhoomi movement to build a temple to the deity at the Babri masjid site was divisive. So, when the BJP pamphlets equate the building of the temple with nation-building (*'Mandir nirman se desh nirman'*), they are striking at the secular foundation of India.

Contrary to the BJP's claims, many still believe that the state should be neutral on matters of faith. And the majority echoes Nehru's view that the temples of modern India are its big infrastructure projects. Why, what is Modi's promise of inclusive development, *'sabka saath, sabka vikas'* all about?

Ram Mandir stickers were pasted on the doors of those contributing to the construction of the temple at Ayodhya.

Yet, we are in an era when religion has been weaponised to the extent that even a chief minister is heckled with slogans of *'Jai Shri Ram'* with the PM watching silently from the dais.

The climate of fear in which dissenters, from students to septuagenarians, are being locked away for years without a trial, also deters non-conformism. All this emboldens the donation seekers to question the religion and patriotism of Hindus who disagree with them when it should be the other way around.

Gated societies, which are so paranoid about access control that they didn't even let in census enumerators, have no compunctions about 'Ram *sevaks*' entering and knocking at every door.

Who wants to be singled out when an FIR is the ruling dispensation's First Instrument of Revenge? They can nab you from any part of India and deposit you in a dungeon in Delhi.

Would these gated societies have let in volunteers seeking donations for the reconstruction of the Babri masjid? That's legitimate too but no one even dare talk about it. On the other hand, the Ram 'bhakts' boast that even Muslims have contributed towards the temple.

Some housing societies are sending requests for donation on their letterheads with the reminder that even the President of India has contributed for the temple. They even keep tabs on who has paid and who hasn't. Messages are circulated by such societies naming those who haven't, giving them another opportunity to donate to a 'national cause'. Big brother and the thought police are here.

For those who have lived through the 'Mandir wahin banayenge' campaign which insisted on building a temple on the mosque site, this is reminiscent of the aftermath of the Babri masjid demolition when the lumpen, armed with electoral rolls, hunted Muslims residents of upmarket South Mumbai localities. In fact, Muslim-owned establishments were torched, including those right outside police stations; a precursor to Gujarat-2002.

Such was the terror that posh housing societies in Mumbai removed the name plates of Muslim occupants, who took the cue and fled to safer areas till sanity returned. Nonetheless their apartments were marked with a 'chand-sitara' (crescent moon and star) sign. Today, the Hindutva brigade is marking the houses of the non-contributors by not pasting a Ram Mandir sticker on the door. The others with stickers can mark themselves as safe.

Even those who question the need for a door-to-door collection drive when the Shri Ram Janambhoomi Teerth Kshetra Trust itself admits to having received more than Rs 1,500 cr in donations, think it prudent to fob off the fund-raisers with a hundred rupee note lest they be targeted. The Ram mandir sticker on their door marks out another victim of intimidatory majoritarianism.

Actually, it is ironic that we are collecting funds for a temple in the middle of a pandemic when these shrines offer no succour, some such as Tirupati even sacked employees. No amount of 'mantra jaap' (reciting hymns) or showering flowers or ringing bells helped where COVID was concerned.

Incidentally, how are people being allowed to go door to door when COVID cases are on the rise again?

The need of the hour is to fund mass vaccination, to build more public hospitals and to increase the health budget which remains 1.5% of the GDP, the fourth-lowest in the world.

Babies die like flies in our hospitals for lack of oxygen cylinders, as in Gorakhpur, or are charred to death because of faulty incubators, as in the Bhandara civil hospital in Maharashtra recently but we are obsessed with a temple for Ram *'lalla'* (the infant Ram).

So gullible are we that even gangsters like Chhota Rajan exploit our religious sentiments. For years, he erected a spectacular Ganeshotsav pandal which drew lakhs of devotees. The display of clout boosted his extortion rates.

The gangster was forced to scale down the pandal when Justice A P Bhangale, then with the MCOCA special court, took *suo motu* notice of an investigative report by yours truly and ordered an inquiry into the funding of the pandal.

The police ought to take notice of the fund-raising for the Ram temple given the fear it has generated. After all, the failure of the Mumbai police to curb the *'maha aartis'* on the streets was one of the reasons why the post-Babri violence spread so fast.

At the end of the day it is a political decision but the governments in non-BJP states are either looking the other way or starting their own fund-raising drives for the Ram temple.

The donation drive is basically an outreach program of the BJP for the next general elections. It also serves to keep the focus away from the mismanagement of the economy, foreign policy and of the country itself.

The Hindutva agenda can be rammed through (no pun intended) and critics can be silenced but if a temple can usher in Ram *rajya*, it would have happened long ago with the reconstruction of the Somnath temple.

✳ ✳ ✳

Section 3

Hatriotism

Choose Between Gandhi and Godse

'Nathuram Godse Zindabad' was trending on Twitter on the morning of October 2, 2020.

Who could have imagined that on his 152nd birth anniversary Mohandas Karamchand Gandhi would have to share the spotlight with Nathuram Godse? The denigration of the man who led the Indian freedom struggle and the glorification of the Hindu zealot who assassinated him has become an industry. Social media is full of posts cursing and abusing Gandhi. Graduates from the WhatsApp University gleefully forward posts about minutiae from his life to somehow show him in a bad light, the context being immaterial.

Gandhi is blamed for Partition, for the execution of Bhagat Singh, for appeasing Muslims and even for the mess that India is in. Godse, on the other hand, is lauded as a nationalist Hindu, a patriot, a hero who slayed a demon. Even Bhagat Singh would come second to him.

So much so that 'Nathuram Godse Zindabad' was trending on Twitter on the morning of October 2, 2020. By evening though, the hashtag 'Gandhi Jayanti' had overtaken Godse; 2.63 lakh to 1.17 lakh. A candidate from Bhopal who hailed Godse as a patriot was elected to Parliament where she repeated the assertion.

The Akhil Bharatiya Hindu Mahasabha, a right-wing Hindu nationalist outfit, celebrates January 30, the day Gandhi was assassinated, as Shaurya Diwas in honour of Godse, who was one of its members. It even tried to install his bust in its office in Meerut. It's not the loony fringe alone, after the Modi government came to power in 2014, several leaders of the Sangh Parivar have been demanding national recognition as freedom fighters, for the killers of Gandhi.

When the world was celebrating Gandhi's 150th birth anniversary, the Mahasabha enacted his assassination, garlanded Godse's portrait and distributed sweets. No, Pooja Shakun Pandey, the Mahasabha leader behind this act, was not denounced as anti-national, nor was she arrested for sedition or UAPA. Not to be left behind, Vicky Mittal, head of the BJP's IT cell in Indore, demanded that Godse's pistol be put on auction to determine which of the two – Gandhi or Godse – was more popular.

All this was happening even as PM Narendra Modi was in the US, spouting Gandhi and penning a piece on him for *The New York Times*. In the article titled, 'Why India and the World Need Gandhi', he said that Gandhi envisioned Indian nationalism "as one that was never narrow or exclusive but one that worked for the service of humanity". He also invited thinkers, entrepreneurs and tech leaders to take the lead to spread Gandhi's ideas through innovation. '*Organiser*', the English journal of the Rashtriya Swayamsevak Sangh (RSS), even dedicated the October 6, 2019 issue to 'Mahatma Gandhi' under the caption, 'Soul of Swaraj'.

So, why the dichotomy? The present regime must choose between Gandhi and Godse. Instead, it tries to appropriate Gandhi even as its policies are at variance with his teachings and even as hardliners continue to rubbish him. Gandhi staked his life to stop the post-Partition Hindu-Muslim riots, something for which the right-wing hardliners hate him. The RSS then wanted all Muslims out of India.

The same kind of hatred is reserved for people like Harsh Mander, who quit the IAS to work for communal harmony after Godhra. Mander, who launched the *Karwan-e-Mohabbat* campaign in solidarity with the victims of communal violence, was sought to be prosecuted for a 'hate speech' in the 2019 Delhi riots. Last month, the Enforcement Directorate searched his offices and home for alleged money laundering. Meanwhile, the man who raised the slogan, '*Desh ke gaddaron ko, goli maro saalon ko* (Shoot the bloody traitors)' at his election rally has become a Union minister.

Academics who refuse to toe the line aren't spared either. Gandhi scholar Rajni Bakshi wrote a piece in *The Indian Express* on October 1 last year on how Gandhi transcended hurt and resentment, channeling the energy into a higher purpose. She was trolled for it.

Except for the odd appreciative letter, the response was an avalanche of abuse, no doubt the handiwork of BJP's hate factory. This is how anyone who is anti-establishment gets labelled as an anti-national, an urban Naxal. This is the kind of sentiment that has resulted in the liquidation of Dabholkar, Pansare, Kalburgi and Gauri Lankesh.

Madhav Sadashiv Golwalkar, RSS leader in its formative years, named Muslims, Christians and Communists respectively as the three biggest 'internal enemies' of the Hindus in India in his 'Bunch of Thoughts' (1966). Historian Ramchandra Guha says the ideology and programme of the RSS can be summarised in six words: We shall show Muslims their place. It is in this light that several people are uneasy with the Partition Horrors Remembrance Day announced by the PM on Independence Day.

The BJP's propaganda machine now produces selective pieces about Gandhi appreciating the selfless work of the RSS. However, the truth is that Gandhi said the RSS was 'communal with a totalitarian outlook'. In fact, Vallabhbhai Patel, whom the RSS juxtaposes with Nehru, was forthright in holding it and the Hindu Mahasabha responsible for creating an environment of hatred against Gandhi which resulted in his assassination. Patel, the first Union home minister, not only condemned the distribution of sweets by certain supporters of the RSS to "celebrate" Gandhi's assassination but also outlawed the organisation and jailed many of its leaders, including Golwalkar, for about a year and a half.

It is not as if Gandhi has not been criticised by his contemporaries and by historians. To elevate him to sainthood and to call him a Mahatma is a bit too much. He was an astute politician but his fancy notions about Hinduism, self-sufficient villages, nature cure and celibacy were not shared by all. Dr Babasaheb Ambedkar was openly critical of Gandhi's endorsement of the caste system. The man had his flaws but his life was an open book, he practised what he preached, never hankered for power and constantly evolved. Not for nothing has he been the inspiration for those swimming against the tide; from Martin Luther King to Ho Chi Minh to Nelson Mandela to Barack Obama.

Mocking Gandhi may be in vogue but walking a mile in his footsteps can transform a fanatic into a follower.

What About *My* Religious Sentiments?

Hindutva is abhorrent for anyone who calls himself a Hindu in the soul-searching tradition of the great rishis.

Writers and artists are walking on eggshells after the Supreme Court declined to grant interim protection from arrest to the makers of the Amazon web series *Tandav*, facing charges of hurting religious sentiments.

Here was a test case of freedom of speech in these trying times but the judges tossed it aside saying that the right to freedom of speech is not absolute. One right that seems to be absolute though is the right to be offended over religion.

In most such cases, merit does not matter and neither do facts. One just has to raise a social media storm, amplify it using pliant media, file FIRs across the country, perform a *'tandav'* outside cinema halls, shops, offices, homes and you have a winner. Your lynch mob is legitimized and those who accuse you of abusing the criminal justice system can be booked under sedition.

The 'religious sentiments' ruse is part of the divisive politics being practiced in our country. The majority community is being constantly fed the lie that their beliefs are being mocked in the name of secularism, that anyone can take liberties with their religion, that Hinduism is in danger.

Netaji Subhas Bose, whom the BJP is trying to appropriate, was a devout Hindu but he was vehemently opposed to the divisive politics of the Hindu Mahasabha. Had he been around today, he would have certainly asked, "What about my religious sentiments?"

It is time to ask how someone sold the majority community the idea that a religion that has withstood the onslaught of Buddhism, Islam and Christianity is in danger of losing its identity. Hinduism is not in danger but the economy is, our democracy is, our jobs are. In fact, the Tirupati temple sacked many of its employees during the lockdown.

The way religion has been weaponised to suit political ends is insulting for anyone who calls himself a Hindu in the soul-searching tradition of the great rishis. Yet, how many *Shankaracharyas* do you see taking offense at it and castigating politicians for hijacking their religion?

How was this concept about the unfinished agenda of Partition re-planted in our minds after seventy years of coexistence, after fighting four wars shoulder-to-shoulder, after our great victories over hunger, disease and illiteracy?

Every sixth Indian is a Muslim; this country has more Muslims than Pakistan has. Forget the unjustness of it, can we imagine the consequences of this divisive line of thought when the temporary migration of a few million workers from cities to villages crippled the country.

Are we blind to the havoc civil strife and religious fundamentalism have created in our neighbourhood? Look at Pakistan's GDP which is a fraction of India's, look at the way it is in the grip of China, look at the lack of religious freedom there, look at the status of its women… Why then are we hell-bent on becoming a mirror image of that failed state? Will slogans such as Hindi-Hindu-Hindustan take us anywhere but to '*kabristan*'.

How did the world's largest democracy which prides itself in its ancient civilization, its robust institutions and its technological prowess come to such a pass? Instead of worshipping at the temples of modern India, we have reverted to stone structures, the very same shrines which came a cropper in COVID. Yet, people are being told to contribute, not to the fight against Covid but to the construction of the Ram temple at Ayodhya.

On the one hand, India uses atomic fission to generate energy and is a proud member of the elite nuclear club and on the other hand a political party in the land of Buddha and Gandhi uses negative energy from societal fission to propel itself to power.

Are lynch mobs our answer to the alleged appeasement of Muslims by the Congress? Does storming college campuses with iron rods fit into the tradition of debate started by Adi Shankara and carried forward by the likes of Vivekananda and Gandhi? Is the creation of a Hindu Taliban the only way of asserting our religious identity?

It is time we examined our deep-rooted biases and the shallow, ritualistic manner in which we practice our religion.

If it were not for our bias, no amount of hate factories would have sold us such blatant lies that we have internalized and that have ultimately led us to believe that the BJP is the saviour of the Hindus.

For us, the Mughals are Islamic invaders when the fact is that they settled down here and enriched the country with their architecture, music, cuisine not to talk of a stable revenue and political system.

We vilify them for destroying temples and for forcible conversion when most of the misconception originates from distortion by colonial historians to present the British as distinct and more civilized rulers than the Mughals. After all, divide-and-rule was their legacy, not that of the Mughals whose interests lay in a syncretic society.

As for the way we practice our religion, we have lost its essence which is compassion. We pour milk over the idols but ignore the malnourished child outside, we offer gold to the deity for wishes fulfilled but have nothing to offer to charity, we even bribe our way to a 'darshan.'

Perhaps this is what Tagore meant when he said, 'Let my country awake' into that heaven of freedom… where the clear stream of reason has not lost its way into the dreary desert sand of dead habit'.

As for the Vedas, the repository of ancient wisdom and metaphysics holds several universal truths and sage advice but they were largely applicable to that day and age. To quote them out of context and claim that ancient India had airplanes to cosmetic surgery to nuclear physics is a mockery of the great texts.

But the worst aspect of *'sanatan dharma'* or the eternal order that is Hinduism is the way its pontiffs accept the inequities of society instead of challenging the status quo. God may not be with the mighty but godmen certainly are.

When the vast majority of Hindus is not vocal about the bad practices that have crept into the religion, imagine how difficult it must be for rationalist Muslims to challenge the *mullas* who filled the vacuum left by the migration of a significant part of their middle class to Pakistan.

A house is built painstakingly, brick-by-brick but those who go around demolishing structures and institutions in the name of nation-building don't realize the harm they are doing.

Ours is still a fragile society and it doesn't take only religion for two groups to come to each other's throats; it could be over sharing of river water between two states, over parochial issues or even a pandemic like COVID.

We have to end this bigotry and hatred because if we don't learn to live together, we will certainly die together.

The Toxic Prime Time News

Stand-up comics speak the truth while TV news anchors conduct cock fights.

Are the two things connected: the decision by Parle and Bajaj Auto not to advertise in shrill TV news channels and the trolling of the Tanishq TV spot?

The former is about toxic news while the latter is about an advertisement that right-wing trolls on social media have deemed toxic to *'Bharatiya sanskriti'*. As with all other things in these polarized times, the answer to whether there is a link between the two depends not on logic but on faith.

If you are not a *'bhakt'* of PM Narendra Modi or even if you are apolitical, chances are that you see a cause and effect; the push-back against toxic news leading to a counter-attack by the saffron brigade on the secular brigade. In fact, chances are that you may have missed all this as you have stopped watching prime time news, disgusted with the hate, hype and hypocrisy.

If you are a Modi fan, you will certainly see a plot by the 'sickulars' and the 'libtards' to defame India and derail its first Hindu ruler in 800 years. You will see the hand of the *'tukde-tukde'* gang in the use of advertisements, such as the one by jewelry brand Tanishq, in promoting *'love jihad'*, allegedly a concerted effort by Muslim men to marry Hindu women and convert them to Islam.

The advertisement by Tanishq, a Tata company, shows a pregnant Hindu wife of a Muslim man being pampered by her mother-in-law who organises her 'baby shower', a ceremony not observed by Muslims. Among the thousands of trolls who found it offensive was actor Kangana Ranaut who said it promoted *love jihad*.

Although the advertisement won widespread praise for depicting India's syncretic culture at a time when news TV channels are stoking Islamophobia, the Tatas pulled it out the same day "keeping in mind the hurt sentiments and the well-being of our employees, partners and store staff".

Just a couple of days prior to this, industrialist Rahul Bajaj had said he would be pulling out advertisements from 'toxic media channels' because he did not want his child to 'inherit an India built on hate'.

Despite the capitulation by the oldest corporate house in India, Tanishq showrooms in Rajkot, Indore and other towns faced hostility and even had to apologise for the advertisement.

The message is clear: Ram *rajya* and '*sabka saath, sabka vikas*' are just '*jumlas*', the rule of law is an alien concept; lynch mobs will rule the streets and troll armies will rule the information highways. The Constitution be damned, majoritarianism rules.

By this logic, M K Gandhi too should be erased from Indian history because the top trend on Twitter this October 2 was not 'Mahatma Gandhi *zindabad*' but 'Nathuram Godse *zindabad*'. Well, the Twitter trends algorithm can be gamed and Gandhians can be shamed.

It does not matter who these trolls are; they could be the Class XII student from Mundra in Gujarat who was arrested for threatening to rape M S Dhoni's infant daughter following his poor form at the ongoing IPL tournament or the MBBS student from Mumbai who threatened the city's police commissioner Parambir Singh, influenced by rants against him on Republic TV.

One is not even talking of threats and abuses faced by critics of the government. Sadly, even the PM follows some such trolls.

It also does not matter if the ratings that drive TV news content are rigged, as the TRP scam being investigated by the Mumbai police shows. This is how the Sushant Singh Rajput case and the Bollywood drugs story take precedence over the pandemic, the border situation with China and the economic crisis.

If you go by the troll army, there is something called '*UPSC jihad*' as well; Muslims 'infiltrating' the civil services. Recently, the Supreme Court had to be petitioned to stop TV channel *Sudarshan News* from airing an episode on *UPSC jihad*.

These are the kind of people who were upset over the Tanishq advertisement as it contradicts the ruling dispensation's vilification of Muslims. And these people can go any extent, including spreading fake news on social media about a non-existent "Muslim Regiment" of the Indian Army refusing to fight in the 1965 war against Pakistan.

The way TV news is competing with Netflix crime thrillers, the way mundane happenings are being labelled 'breaking news', the degeneration of debates into cock-fights, and the partisan approach of the anchors all add to a toxic environment. No wonder that Congress spokesperson Rajiv Tyagi died of a heart attack soon after a TV debate.

The trash that passes as news on TV is proof that journalism has gone out of journalists' hands. Decisions are taken by finance managers in search of revenue; hence advertorials, infotainment, paid news, fake news, clickbait journalism, conspiracy theories, jingoism, Islamophobia; anything but news. The prize for hypocrisy goes to *Sudarshan News* which defended its *UPSC jihad* in the Supreme Court in the name of investigative journalism.

A meme sums up the situation:'The news used to tell us what happened and we had to decide how we felt about it. Now the news tells us how to feel and we have to decide if it happened.'

Instead of leaders of thought, editors have become production managers with titles such as Editor (Mumbai market) to remind them of their responsibility to the bottom line. They have even ceded the editorial page to politicians. With shrinking budgets and the sheen of the profession having worn off, journalism is no longer attracting the talent it used to. Young idealists join the media hoping to change the world but quit when they realize they can't even change a word.

Republic TV's J&K bureau chief Tejinder Singh Sodhi revealed in his resignation letter that the *Republic TV* team in Delhi was not allowed to cover a major Congress press conference. Instead, he wrote, we were asked to protest outside the Congress office in our respective states by wearing black bands.

Media houses have pompous taglines, such as, 'the leader guards the reader' when they throw their own correspondents to the wolves at the first sign of trouble. This is the reason for self-censorship. No wonder the profession now attracts youngsters who can't distinguish a policeman from a postman outside Kangana's Bandra office, who came to blows with each other outside the office of the Narcotics Control Bureau. Everyone except the viewer is asked, "*Aap ko kaisa lag raha hai?*"

Media houses claim to 'afflict the comfortable and comfort the afflicted' and 'speak truth to power' when the reality is that stand-up comics speak more truth than journalists.

The real news of today is how dissent is being criminalized, how RTI is being strangled, how the mainstream media botoxifies the ugly truth, and how journalists uncovering lies are being hounded and arrested. No one mentions it but the liberal use of sedition to silence critics is part of the Gujarat model.

To end, a Turkish joke: A political prisoner goes to the jail's library to ask for a book. The librarian says, we don't have the book but we have its author.

✳ ✳ ✳

Hindi & Urdu Are Like Sisters

Urdu belongs to the composite culture of India.

Those who saw a clothing firm's catchline, 'Jashn-e-Riwaaz', as an attempt to 'abrahamise' Hindu festivals recently were left speechless when noted writer Javed Akhtar pointed out that three of the four words in the BJP's slogan for the UP Assembly polls – '*Soch imaandar, kaam dumdaar*' — came from Urdu; *imaandar, kaam* and *dumdaar*.

So, the Hindutva troll army went after the language instead. Sample a couple of printable responses, typical of the '*bhakt*'. The first is denial: "Urdu is no language at first place. The verbs used in entire Urdu are 100% taken from Hindi which in turn comes from Sanskrit. Without verbs there can be no language. Urdu is no language. I repeat Urdu is no language."

The second is a conspiracy theory: "I always wondered what was the need to invent Urdu when India already had so many rich languages!! Is it not part of an agenda? Why West Pakistan tried to impose Urdu on East Pakistan and ended up losing it and also massacring millions of Bangla speakers?"

The misconception is that Urdu is a Pakistani language, that it is the language of the Islamic invaders. With their warped sense of history, these bigots see Urdu as a vestige of centuries of subjugation. Hence, its demonisation. These ignoramuses should hear Urdu scholar Gopichand

Narang: "Urdu is not the language of Muslims. If at all there is any language of Muslims, it should be Arabic. Urdu belongs to the composite culture of India. Hindi and Urdu are supplementary and complementary. They are like sisters strengthening each other."

These graduates of the WhatsApp University are not taught that Upendranath Sharma 'Ashk' and Dhanpat Rai Srivastava, better known as Munshi Premchand, were famous Urdu authors before they even began to write in Hindi, that Urdu literature has been overwhelmingly patronised by non-Muslim writers and poets: Krishan Chander, Rajinder Singh Bedi, Raghupati Sahay (Firaq Gorakhpuri), Gulzar (Sampooran Singh Kalra), Khushwant Singh... *Rekhta.org*, possibly the most comprehensive site on Urdu, is run by a Marwari Hindu.

The vilification of Urdu is part of a sectarian campaign that springs from the misplaced ideology of the late Guru Golwalkar of the Rashtriya Swayamsevak Sangh (RSS), who believed that the "non-Hindu people of Hindustan must either adopt Hindu culture and language, must learn and respect and hold in reverence the Hindu religion, must entertain no idea but of those of glorification of the Hindu race and culture..."

The Prime Minister chooses to speak in Sanskritised Hindi on important occasions. For instance, this I-Day, he used terms such as *'paavan parv', 'naman', 'nyochhavar', 'kaalkhand', 'samarpit', 'itihas'...* However, one Sanskrit word which he eschewed was *'mitron'.* Subscribers to the Hindi-Hindu-Hindustan ideology will be surprised to learn that former Maharashtra CM Devendra Fadnavis' surname is derived from two Persian words, *'farad'* and *'navis'*; it translates into English as 'maker of the lists'.

It does not matter to 'hatriots' that Urdu — an Indic language closely related to Hindi but written in the Persian script and having many loanwords from Persian and Arabic — is one of our officially recognised languages. It is the seventh most spoken language in India. If we were to replace Urdu words with those in Hindi, some of Bollywood's most memorable lines would fall flat: *'Mogambo prasann hua'*; *'Kitne vyakti thay?'*; *'Don ko pakadna kathin he nahin, asambhav hai'*; *'Ye sansaar, ye sammelan mere kaam kay nahin'...*

Which courtroom scene would be complete without *'chashmadeed gawah'*, *'tazeerat-e Hind ke tahat'* and *'ba-izzat bari'*. The word, *'adalat'*, itself is from Urdu. Hindi films and their songs are peppered with *'sukoon'* (peace), *'roohaniyat'* (spirituality), *'mukammal'* (complete), *'justajoo'* (a longing), *'shiddat'* (intensity), *'inayat'* (blessing), *'aafreen'* (alluring)… Not to mention *'Woh yaar ho jo khushboo ki tarah/ Jiski zubaan Urdu ki tarah'* from Gulzar's *'Chaiyaa, chaiyya…'* set to music by A R Rahman in the Mani Ratnam film, *'Dil Se'*. Indeed, Urdu sounds so poetic and so dignified that the uninitiated may feel flattered even when they are being insulted.

It is another matter that Bollywood is losing touch with Urdu. Today's scriptwriters do not have the same command over the language as their forebears and the actors lack the impeccable delivery of yesteryear's stars. One can say that the *'dumdaar'* dialogues of someone like Dilip Kumar are missing. However, there's something positive too. A yet-to-be-released Hindi film, *'Sehar'*, by debutant Munzir Naqvi deals with the engineered demonization of Urdu. The film's protagonist, an Urdu professor played by Pankaj Kapur, struggles to save his course in the face of diminishing enrolment, poor funding, and a general belief that a degree in Urdu isn't suited for the workplace.

Until Independence, Urdu was widely spoken in North India and within the bureaucracy. But after Partition the language became increasingly associated with Islam and Pakistan. So complete was the communal association of Hindi and Urdu by that time that Urdu made it to the Constitution as part of a largely perfunctory list of official languages, only because Prime Minister Nehru insisted on it.

In 1955, an Official Languages Commission was appointed by the Union government to coin modern Hindi words, given that it was going to be used for the first time as an administrative language. The late Hindi poet Harivansh Rai Bachchan describes in his autobiography the amazement the incomprehensible Sanskritic neologisms caused; a radio was *'vidyut prasaran'* and a train, *'lauhpath gamini'*.

The politics of Hindi-Urdu division is not new, it stretches back to the 19th century. Fortunately, the politics of Hindi-Urdu unity too has roots going back as far. Poet and satirist Akbar Allahabadi captured the fake fight in these lines, still relevant a century later:

Hum Urdu ko Arabi kyon na karein
Hindi ko voh Bhasha (Sanskrit) kyon na karein
Jhagre ke liye akhbaron mein mazmun tarasha kyon na karein
Aapas mein adavat kuch bhi nahin lekin ek akhara qaim hai
Jab is se falak ka dil behle hum log tamasha kyon na karein

(Why shouldn't we turn Urdu into Arabic and Hindi into Bhasha? Why shouldn't we write divisive articles in newspapers to fuel the fight? There is no mutual animosity but an arena is prepared: Why shouldn't we make a scene, when this cheers the heart of the heavens?)

Section 4

Men in the Muddle

Corona and the Accidental Chief Minister

The wonder is how Uddhav has managed to use his handicaps to his advantage.

Delhi was expected to do better than Mumbai in handling the pandemic; it has a popular CM in Arvind Kejriwal, model *mohalla* clinics and the vast resources of a national capital whereas Mumbai has an accidental CM in Uddhav Thackeray, it is unbelievably crowded and filthy and the capital of a state starved of funds by the Centre.

Initially, Mumbai lagged far behind Delhi. Yet, like the proverbial tortoise, Mumbai has overtaken Delhi. On November 19, the number of active cases in Delhi stood at 43,221 whereas the figure for Mumbai was 11,694.

Maharashtra, which accounted for a quarter of the corona cases and half the deaths at the beginning, has managed to bring its caseload down and is the only one in the top-five worst-hit states where the number of active cases is going down.

Part of the credit for this goes to Uddhav Thackeray, who completes one year as CM today. He has been a revelation. Here's a man whose interest lay in photography rather than in politics, who had no administrative experience and who has eight stents in his heart. To top it, the man has the charisma of a bank clerk.

Eknath Shinde next to Uddhav Thackeray at the latter's swearing-in ceremony. Credit: Prashant Nakwe

The wonder is how Uddhav has managed to use his handicaps to his advantage. To begin with, he lacked a first-hand knowledge of how the bureaucracy functions, having never held a public post. The bureaucracy is a bull that bucks its riders; Uddhav's predecessor Devendra Fadnavis fulminated against babus till the end of his term.

To everyone's surprise, Uddhav decided to continue with Ajoy Mehta, chief secretary under Fadnavis, now the leader of the Opposition. Uddhav gave Mehta a free hand. When Pravin Pardeshi, who wasn't doing a bad job as Mumbai municipal commissioner, clashed with Mehta, he was replaced. Uddhav got it right; in any war, there can be only one general and this is a war against COVID.

The Uddhav-Mehta duo acted decisively; enforcing a strict lockdown, going to the extent of impounding cars, marking out containment zones and most importantly, systematically gathering reliable data. Senior civic officials were assigned tasks and the slackers were shunted out.

Uddhav's alliance partners in the Maha Vikas Aghadi accused Mehta of acting as the super CM, but to no avail. Not that the duo made no mistakes but they were rectified quickly. The one-general policy has paid off. One of the early successes was the containment of COVID in Dharavi, Asia's largest slum.

This is not to say that Uddhav does not step in when he realizes that things are going wrong. Responding to widespread complaints about the indiscriminate use of force by cops he told them to use their *lathis* judiciously.

It is easy for a new and beleaguered CM to give in to the temptation of populism. To his credit, Uddhav resisted it. Schools, malls, cinema halls and eateries remained shut; even roadside *vadapav* stalls were not permitted despite a nudge by Shiv Sena leader Sanjay Raut. "I am not Trump," Uddhav told him.

Unlike Delhi's metro which resumed in September, local trains in Mumbai carry only those running essential services. Bus services started in Mumbai in June while the intra-state services resumed in August.

Delhi opened temples, mosques, etc. in June but Mumbai held on till November despite jibes by the BJP. Maharashtra governor Koshiyari even twisted the knife, wondering aloud whether Uddhav had turned 'secular'.

Given the Shiv Sena's past and its role in the post-Babri communal riots, Uddhav went out of his way to reassure Muslims; the guardian minister of Mumbai is Aslam Shaikh of the Congress. The community reciprocated by heeding the CM's call not to allow congregations in mosques.

In fact, the Shiv Sena mouthpiece *Saamna* carried an editorial questioning the utility of shrines in a pandemic. However, Uddhav's cousin Raj Thackeray, whose Maharashtra Navnirman Sena won just one seat in the last assembly polls, sought to stoke the anti-Muslim sentiment during the Tablighi Jamaat episode.

Here too Uddhav stepped in to curb hate messages. By April, 196 cases had been registered across the state against fake news, rumours and hate speech, with 37 arrests, including that of a man who threatened a state cabinet minister with the fate of Narendra Dabholkar.

Uddhav makes up for his lack of charisma by his earnestness. No *jumlas* like Modi, no rhetoric like his late father Bal Thackeray, he believes in plainspeak. The CM neither hypes nor hides anything in his daily briefings, stating the facts with figures; the number of patients, number of deaths, hotspot areas, preparedness on the part of the government in terms of the number of hospitals and hospital beds, etc.

Even experts agree that Mumbai, unlike Delhi, routinely puts out all its Covid-related data for the world to see. The daily bulletins issued by the BMC run into multiple pages, offering granular data, while those of Delhi are one-pagers.

Citizens have appreciated Uddhav's sincerity, frankness, inclusivity, firmness and an unbiased approach in the fight against Covid. He has also avoided a blame game with the Centre or a slanging match with Fadnavis. The Dhoni-like 'keep calm and carry on' approach is paying dividends.

Such is the faith in his word that people with symptoms opt to go to one of the jumbo facilities set up by the government instead of rushing to private hospitals. Ganeshotsav, Navratri and Diwali were remarkably low-key although Diwali shopping crowds at Dadar were alarming.

All the while, Uddhav Thackeray has been working from home but behind the scenes, the man who has made life easy for him is the wily NCP leader Sharad Pawar. Thanks to him, the three-party alliance has remained free of friction and Deputy CM Ajit Pawar has uncharacteristically kept a low profile.

The MVA responded to the BJP's oft-repeated threat to topple it by engineering the defection of senior BJP leader Eknath Khadse. Instead of Operation Kamal, Maharashtra witnessed Operation Khadse. Thus Uddhav's challenge to Fadnavis at his party's annual Dussera rally: Don't just talk, do it.

However, the threat is real. There is growing resentment in the Shiv Sena about Uddhav's coterie and the way his son Aditya is being foisted on the party. Satraps such as Eknath Shinde and Diwakar Raote, who enjoy the support of a sizable section of the MLAs, feel sidelined and could be lured away from the Shiv Sena.

Politics is like a T20 game of cricket these days. It can change any moment. Uddhav has hit a slew of boundaries in the first six overs where only two fielders are allowed outside the inner circle but his strike rate is bound to dip when the field spreads out.

✳ ✳ ✳

Nana Phadnavis to Devendra Fad-novice?

Which Chanakya would use a pandemic to score political points.

Devendra Fadnavis has a famous surname. For a while, he was even compared favourably with the man who made it famous — Nana Phadnavis, the Chanakya of the Maratha empire. Today, however, the resonance is lost. Let alone Chanakya, the man isn't doing justice even to the post of Leader of the Opposition in a state where he was the CM.

Which Chanakya would stoop to soap operas starring Sushant Singh Rajput's girlfriend or Kangana Ranaut? Or bank on lapdog channels such as *Republic TV*? Using a pandemic to score points is no political punditry either.

Although both are Maharashtrian brahmins, Fadnavis shares no kinship with his historical namesake; he is a *'Deshastha'*, a community whose roots are in central India, whereas Nana Phadnavis was a *'Chitpawan'*, who come from coastal Maharashtra; Velas near Shrivardhan to be precise.

To begin with, Phadnavis was not a surname. It was the office of the finance minister under the Peshwas. Derived from two Persian words, *'farad'* and *'navis'*, it translates into English as 'maker of the lists'.

The Peshwas, brahmins again, began as ministers but eventually took over the reins by disempowering Shivaji's successors. Nana Phadnavis, born

Balaji Janardan Bhanu, was not merely the chancellor but the *de facto* ruler of the Maratha Empire in the late 18th century.

Under him, the Marathas held sway from the Kumaon hills in the north to the Cauvery river in the South and from Gujarat to Odisha. To the British, whom he kept at bay for three decades, Nana Phadnavis was the Maratha Machiavelli.

The only Machiavellian move by Devendra Fadnavis has been the marginalization of his rivals as well as potential rivals in the BJP once the Modi-Shah duo chose him as the CM in 2014 over established leaders such as Nitin Gadkari and Eknath Khadse.

Fadnavis has changed so much since then that it is impossible to recognize him. Earlier as an opposition leader, he charmed the media, cornering the Congress government in TV debates as well as in the assembly. Today, he is behaving like a sore loser; getting into slanging matches with second-rung Sena leader Sanjay Raut and predicting the demise of the Maha Vikas Aghadi (MVA) government on a monthly basis.

He even called for President's rule to be imposed in Maharashtra since 'dissenters' such as Arnab Goswami of *Republic TV* and Kangana Ranaut were sought to be silenced. The irony of 'urban Naxals', such as Sudha Bharadwaj, Anand Teltumbde and Fr Stan Swamy, is lost on him.

This is the same man who spoke softly and spoke sense. Today, he yells at the top of his voice, replacing debate with demagoguery. As opposition leader, he went after the Adarsh and the irrigation scams but as CM he used them as bargaining chips.

In fact, Fadnavis reminds one of the central characters in the 1985 Marathi musical *Padgham*; a student leader who goes from clenched fist to folded hands as he metamorphoses into a politician, making compromise after compromise to head the very system he had rebelled against.

Incidentally, Fadnavis was a student leader. He was just 21 when he was elected corporator, 27 when he became mayor of Nagpur and 44 when he became the CM.

Nana Phadnavis checkmated enemies though his legendary network of spies, Fadnavis has his friends in the media who helped him slander party rivals; Khadse, Vinod Tawde, Pankaja Munde, all were embroiled in controversies. The first two did not even get party tickets in the 2019 polls while Pankaja, daughter of the late Gopinath Munde, lost to her cousin, Dhananjay Munde of the NCP.

The same coterie of court poets built up Fadnavis' profile. Today, it is difficult to think of a rival to him in the state BJP.

Given the Peshwa history, Fadnavis is aware that Maratha chieftains cannot digest a brahmin CM. He rubbed it in by getting Sambhaji Raje, the 13th direct descendent of Shivaji, nominated to the Rajya Sabha in 2016. Sharad Pawar retorted by harking back to the times when the Maratha Chhatrapati would appoint a Peshwa (chief minister), who in turn would choose a Fadnavis; "I hadn't witnessed a Fadnavis appointing a Chhatrapati until now."

As CM, he was too busy to govern; he was plotting against rivals and emulating Modi by campaigning for the party, even in municipal elections. Fadnavis' flagship project, the *Jalyukt Shivar Abhiyan*, did little to tackle drought and increase groundwater level despite the approximately Rs 10,000 cr sunk in it. The Comptroller and Auditor-General also slammed the scheme for its lack of transparency. The MVA government has since scrapped the scheme and decided to probe the irregularities in it.

At that time though, Fadnavis seemed invincible. So much so that senior Congress leaders Radhakrishna Vikhe Patil and Harshvardhan Patil and a host of top NCP leaders defected to the BJP, including another Shivaji descendent Udayan Raje Bhosale.

So confident was he that Modi's charisma would sweep the BJP back to power in Maharashtra that Fadnavis roared in each of his rallies that he would return as CM; "*Me punha yein*". He even taunted Sharad Pawar, saying that the NCP lacked the stomach for a fight.

Nana Phadnavis was never so cocky. He was a team player who joined hands with 11 other chieftains to depose the unpopular Peshwa Raghunathrao in 1774. To fend off the British, he forged tactical alliances even with the Nizam of Hyderabad and the Nawab of Arcot.

This arrogance cost Fadnavis dearly in 2019 when the BJP, which was confident of improving on its 2014 assembly poll tally of 122 seats, won just 105 seats. Sharad Pawar's NCP won 54 seats, 14 seats more than the last time. The Maratha chieftain showed that he had the guts for a fight. Soon, Fadnavis was to learn that the wily Maratha had a game plan as well. The true Phadnavis taught a lesson to the Fad-novice.

The 1979 Marathi classic *Simhasan* directed by Jabbar Patel and written by Arun Sadhu, who also penned *Padgham*, pales before the twists and turns in the post-poll drama in 2019. Three young journalists have written books on it; Sudhir Suryavanshi (*Checkmate*), Jitendra Dixit (*35 Days*) and Kamesh Sutar (*36 Days*). It will be most surely be milked by Bollywood.

However, it is by no means the end for Devendra Fadnavis who has time on his side. He can also take heart from the fact that his namesake survived the humiliating defeat of the Marathas at the battle of Panipat in 1761 and went on to restore the might of the Maratha Empire.

*** * ***

Section 5

Reimagining Mumbai

The City of Gold Must Sparkle

Mumbai is a vivacious young woman with a bad dress-sense and messy make-up.

A Bollywood actress says something about Mumbai and the Shiv Sena takes the bait but earlier this month when the Union government right royally snubbed Mumbai over the Clean City awards, no one even reacted to it.

Navi Mumbai, the Maximum City's 'bedroom suburb', was declared the third cleanest city in India in the Swachh Survekshan but Mumbai, ranked 18th overall nationwide in 2018, failed to make it to the top hundred. Ouch! You have been told that your outhouse is cleaner than your bungalow. Kangana Ranaut couldn't have conjured up such an insult.

Now, let's look at the facts. Navi Mumbai is half the size of Mumbai but with just six per cent of its population. Besides, it's a planned city. Mumbai, given its congestion, is not doing a bad job on the cleanliness front. Having lived in Mumbai for nearly half a century and in Navi Mumbai for a decade now, I can say with authority that window-dressing rather than any hard-scrubbing has got the satellite city the ranking.

Mumbai has all it takes to be a beautiful city; the sea and the sandy stretches, the lakes and the lagoons, the hills and the forests, the glitz and the glamour, the moolah and the magic… And unlike other metros, Mumbai comes into its own at night.

The problem however is that the city is unable to project itself; it's a vivacious young woman with a bad dress-sense and messy make-up.

Take the iconic Marine Drive bay which just a handful of cities in the world are blessed with. It is supposed to have been beautified with help from a business tycoon but it looks like chrome plating on an antique masterpiece; just as ugly as that man's house. How can one talk of aesthetics when full-grown trees on the Marine Drive promenade were hacked in the name of renovation.

Look at where Marine Drive ends, a concrete jumble of office blocks called Nariman Point, an ugly monument to greed. To make it worse, we squeezed in the Vidhan Bhavan. The government could have learnt from the previous such exercise at creating a Central Business District just 50 years ago, Ballard Estate. Today, this European style office precinct is in neglect; a beautiful pendant waiting for a necklace.

In the same area, D N Road, which leads from the World Heritage Structure of Chhatrapati Shivaji Maharaj Terminus to Flora Fountain, has improved of late, thanks to the efforts of a conservation architect who lobbied to get the Neoclassical and Gothic Revival buildings restored and shrunk the signboards on them. Yet, if your gaze falls on the blue plastic raincoats on the domes of the GPO building, the heritage halo of the CSMT precinct dissipates in a flash. We are simply unable to take a holistic view of things.

There was a time when British tourists took a tree tour of the city in *tongas*. Now, the island city has lost almost all of the pre-Independence era foliage to road widening and digging for the metro; thank God the maidans are still intact. The replacement trees, fast-growing exotic varieties such the Peltophorum and Gulmohur, have shallow roots and fall like ninepins in monsoon gales.

The biggest spoiler in Mumbai are its narrow and clogged roads. If it has to make an impression, Mumbai must first unclog and then spruce up its highways, central avenues, skywalks and approach roads to railway stations. Wider pedestrian walkways, designated spaces for hawkers, uniformity in street furniture, flower beds, clean public toilets and some quality art installations. Is this too much to ask for?

The streets need a canopy of native flowering trees such as the Indian Laburnum, the Pride-of-India and the Bauhinia (*Kachar*), not hoardings blocking the sun. It is a tragedy that no one knows of efforts such as the Bakul avenue created by Dr Ashok Kothari of the BNHS at SNDT Women's University at Santa Cruz.

Best Tree/Garden/Avenue awards ought to be instituted in every suburb. Yes, money grows on trees where image-building is concerned. And for God's sake, why can't the richest municipal corporation in India get jet sprays to clean the trees of the dust and the grime. Up to the sixties, even the roads were washed.

A mandatory fresh coat of paint on buildings lining the main avenues will go a long way in changing the drab look of the city.

Mumbai does not sanction the use of the space under flyovers for parking but there is no beautification plan for it. A mention must be made here of the Matunga flyover under which local residents have created an innovative garden with a schematic model of the Narmada river. Is it too much for the Brihanmumbai Municipal Corporation (BMC) to replicate it? Where are the corporates who have made their trillions from this city?

The BMC does not take beautification seriously because greening the city is not part of its obligatory duties. Likewise, the railways are unconcerned about cleanliness on the tracks and a dash of greenery at local stations. Come to think of it, why can't 'sarkari' buildings, hospitals, police stations etc be incentivized to maintain greenery on their premises.

Mumbai needs to showcase its strengths. It has done precious little to exploit its seafront and to develop water sports. As in the case of D N Road, it took a private citizen to initiate the cleaning of Versova beach. Forget boat rides from coast to coast, we don't have a marina.

Mangroves are showcased as nature's wonders in other countries with ticketed tours but in Mumbai, they are used exclusively for dumping debris with encroachment in mind. World over, creeks are meant for recreational fishing, boating and water transport; here they are open gutters. The less said the better about Mumbai's four rivers. A beginning of sorts though has been made by declaring the Airoli mangroves in Navi Mumbai as a Flamingo sanctuary.

Despite the negatives, private enterprise and public participation have led to the wonderful transformation of small parcels of land. The Priyadarshini park and the Amarsons garden in South Mumbai to name two. Who would believe that the garden behind Goregaon's Inorbit mall, as good as any in Singapore, was the Chincholi bunder dumping ground or that the Jogger's Park and Band Stand promenade in Bandra were rocky patches abutting the road.

Mumbai, which prides itself as the *Urbs Prima in Indis*, has just 1.24 sq m of accessible open space per person. It missed a big opportunity to improve the open space to population ratio 15 years ago when the mill lands in Central Mumbai opened up for development. Architect Charles Correa, one of the planners of Navi Mumbai, had envisaged a 5-km green corridor running from Mahalaxmi to Parel, but once again greed aced good sense.

However, all is not lost. The compactness of Mumbai can be used to its advantage when it comes to beautification. Look at Surat which went from *'badsurat'* to *'khoobsurat'* in five years. But we must remember to improve slums as well, otherwise the next pandemic will explode in our faces. *Purishapuri*, or toilet city, is a tag we have worked hard to get rid of.

There is a dire need to re-imagine the city, to harness its amazing energy, to tap its immense wealth but for that we need to think straight, think big and have a grand plan. The sugar belt satraps who rule the state have no such dreams. Now, it is for those who have grown up in Mumbai and for those who have grown in Mumbai rather than those who have grown on Mumbai to give back something to the city.

The Shiv Sena with its roots in Mumbai and its hold over the municipal corporation can take it up as their big idea. If it can just forget Kangana and avenge the real insult it will have shown that *'Amchi Mumbai'* is more than just a slogan.

* * *

Celebrating Mumbai's Living Heritage

Mumbai lacks ancient monuments but its World Heritage structures are functional buildings.

A pandemic, a city on the edge, a Russian vaccine! Things have come full circle for Mumbai in 125 years. And what better occasion than the eve of World Heritage Day to bring it up. It would have been a very different Mumbai but for Russian scientist Waldemar Mordecai Haffkine who developed a vaccine for the bubonic plague of 1896 that hit Bombay and Poona.

Room no 000 of Byculla's Grant Medical College, which housed his lab, exists, as does the Portuguese mansion subsequently given to him for research, now the Haffkine Institute in Parel. In fact, one can catch a glimpse of those days in the museum there.

Unlike Delhi, Varanasi or even Ahmedabad, Mumbai is just 300 years old and lacks ancient monuments but it has gems such as Haffkine's Institute; a case of living heritage.

Unfortunately, this blinded us to the true value of our heritage buildings till recently. For instance, rooms came up in the wide verandahs of the Chhatrapati Shivaji Maharaj Terminus (CSMT) building, ugly extensions were made for a canteen, gargoyles knocked out… It never occurred to the occupants, the Central Railway, that this was sacrilege. In fact, so poor was the upkeep that the iconic building leaked in the monsoon; slipshod waterproofing saw tar dripping on the faces set in the walls, one of them being that of philanthropist Jagannath Shankarseth.

Mumbai's `heritage square' looks forlorn during the lockdown.
Credit: Sudharak Olwe

The CSMT started getting the attention it deserves when it was declared a World heritage site in 2004 by UNESCO. Constructed in 1888, the cathedral-like building is an outstanding example of the Victorian Gothic Revival style; Bombay's answer to the Taj Mahal.

The two grand structures flanking the CSMT that house the GPO and the municipality pale in comparison. The former is modelled on the Gol Gumbaz of Bijapur in Karnataka while the latter is a diet version of the CSMT. Both are being botoxed ever since their neighbour won the beauty pageant.

It is not easy to get a world heritage tag; the site must hold an outstanding universal value that is beyond national boundaries and of great significance for future generations.

India has 38 such sites and Mumbai accounts for three of them. While the Elephanta caves, dating back to 2,500 years and predominantly dedicated to Shiva, became a world heritage site in 1987, the cluster of Victorian and Art Deco buildings near the Oval Maidan, barely one km from CSTM, got the tag in 2018. Prominent among the Art Deco structures are the Eros, Regal and Metro theatres and the buildings on Marine Drive.

While we celebrate our world heritage sites, we must also appreciate and conserve the lesser such sites the city has to offer; 591 as of 2012.

Apart from the Elephanta caves, the Mumbai region has 175 caves. Prominent among the ones in the city are the Buddhist Kanheri caves in Borivali national park, visited by Chinese monk Hiuen Tsang in the seventh century, the Mahakali caves at Andheri, the Mandapeshvara caves at Borivali and the Jogeshwari caves, off the Western Express highway.

Jogeshwari, in fact, gets its name from the mother goddess Yogeshwari, one of the deities in the large cave complex. The caves depict several mythological stories; one shows the marriage of Shiva and Parvati while another depicts the couple playing a game of dice.

Till 15 years ago, there was a slum atop the Jogeshwari caves. Had they not been shifted, the beautiful caves would have gone the way of the ones at Magathane, Kandivli, which even the Bombay High Court refused to protect saying that there was nothing left to protect.

Mumbai has four small coastal forts; at Bandra, Mahim, Worli, Sewri, and one atop a hill at Sion. The East India Company built a big fort overlooking the Mumbai harbour. Its walls were pulled down in 1860 and only one small section stands on P D' Mello Road. However, the area from CSMT to the Gateway of India is still called Fort.

Mumbai has heritage precincts such as Khotachiwadi in Girgaon, Matharpacady in Mazgaon and Ranwar village at Bandra which retain the old world charm. On the other hand, it has the forerunner of Nariman Point and the Bandra-Kurla Complex (BKC) in Ballard Estate which has a 'London feel' to it, thanks to its European Renaissance facades.

Mani Bhavan at Gamdevi which hosted Mahatma Gandhi and Rajgruha at Dadar where Babasaheb Ambedkar lived are memorial museums. This is not the case with Sardar Gruha at Crawford Market where Tilak lived and the bungalow in JJ School of Arts where Rudyard Kipling lived as a child.

Apart from the museum and the National Gallery for Modern Art, both at Kala Ghoda, the city boasts of the National Museum on Indian Cinema at Gulshan Mahal, a 19th-century Victorian bungalow at the Films

Division premises in Pedder Road, the Archdiocesan heritage museum at St Pius X college, Goregaon, the Alpaiwalla Parsi museum at Khareghat colony, the Coin museum behind the RBI building, the BEST bus museum at Wadala's Anik depot, the Bombay High Court museum in the building itself and the museum created in the recently discovered bunker below Raj Bhavan, which used to be the British governor's residence. In 2010, a tunnel and hall were found below the GPO too.

Incidentally, the Haffkine Institute used to be the Governor's House. The Prince of Wales was felicitated in its majestic Durbar Hall during his visit in 1875. Since then it is used for public functions and many great scientists like C V Raman have delivered scientific orations here.

Among the museums in the offing are a textile mill museum at Byculla, a maritime museum at the Mumbai Port Trust premises and a police museum at the police commissioner's office. Then there's the sky museum on the 15 to the 18th floor of J K house at Breach Candy which should open once the pandemic is over. A case for a freedom movement heritage circuit including the August Kranti Maidan and Azad Maidan also has been made.

The numerous weekend heritage walks show the growing interest in the topic. Other positive signs are the restoration of the Royal Opera house, the Bhau Daji Lad museum, the Flora fountain, the Banganga tank, the Bandra railway station and the de-cluttering of hoardings on D N Road. Several public buildings such as the CSTM, the BMC, the GPO and the high court are now open to heritage lovers.

All this is because of the efforts of people such as Rahul Mehrotra, Abha Narain Lambah, Vikas Dilawari, Brinda Somaya, Tasneem Mehta and the late Sharada Dwivedi who raised heritage consciousness.

It is now up to citizens to act as the patrons and custodians of Mumbai's heritage. Vocal for local, to quote PM Narendra Modi. For instance, British-era milestones must be protected from encroachers, defacing of heritage structures must not be tolerated and fencing and plaques can be put up at sites.

Leaders also must weigh in. The credit for Ahmedabad being chosen over Delhi and Mumbai as India's first world heritage city in 2017 goes to Narendra Modi who had been working on it for a long time.

Coming back to the Haffkine Institute, in 2015 the BJP-Sena government had approached it to part with three of its 22 acres for the Bal Thackeray memorial. The institute turned down the request saying it needed the space for expansion.

There may have been another reason. In 1996, Shiv Sena goons blackened Haffkine director Vishwanath Yemul's face over 'irregularities' and dragged him to Bal Thackeray's residence at Matoshree.

But in another instance of things coming full circle, his son Uddhav's plea to let the state-owned Haffkine Bio-Pharmaceutical Corporation Ltd manufacture the COVID-19 vaccine has been granted by the Centre.

Maximum City Must Get More Vocal for Its *Local*

Had Mumbai been an independent railway zone, it wouldn't have taken commuters' riots to go from nine-coach to 12-coach trains.

You are not a true blue Mumbai commuter until you have spent a night stranded at the last railway station because you overslept. The solitary agony of the endless wait for the morning train is now shared by the entire city.

Although some trains are running and the list of permitted categories is increasing, no one knows when everyone will be able to board the locals. Last week, scientists at the Tata Institute of Fundamental Research (TIFR) suggested that the authorities needn't be so timid about opening up the local trains given the high antibody positivity in the city and the declining cases of COVID-'19.

Not for nothing are the suburban trains called the lifeline of Mumbai. With tracks spread over 465 km – more than the distance between Pune and back — the Mumbai suburban railway operates 2,342 train services and carries 7.5 million commuters daily, almost one-third of the population of Australia.

The outsider would presume that Mumbai is one of India's 17 railway zones but that is not the case. It is partitioned between two giants; the Western Railway zone and the Central Railway zone. The jurisdiction of the former extends from Churchgate to Ratlam in MP while that of the latter extends from Chhatrapati Shivaji Maharaj Terminus (CSMT) to Nagpur and Solapur. Obviously, Mumbai cannot be the priority for either. Have you ever heard of a public consultation held by the railways with Mumbai commuters?

The absence of effective commuters' organisations and the indifference of political parties to the woes of Mumbai's travelling public have combined to deprive the city of a dedicated railway zone. Political parties are more interested in railway unions, especially the ones concerning loco drivers or motormen that give them the power to paralyse the city with a strike.

Just one of the six MPs from the city attended a rare meeting of parliamentarians called by the railway board chairman in 2012 to discuss Mumbai's issues. The media missed the scoop. The Maximum City certainly needs to get more vocal about the local.

Had Mumbai been an independent railway zone, it wouldn't have taken commuters' riots to go from nine-coach to 12-coach trains, commuters wouldn't have to wait 10 years to get one air-conditioned train, it wouldn't take three years and dozens of deaths to close the huge gap between the footboard of the new trains and the platform.

An overwhelming 55% of Mumbai uses local trains with the average trip length being 26 km, compared to 6.5 km by bus. Only 8% of the taxpaying population own cars.

A Mumbaikar spends anywhere between half an hour to four hours a day in the local train as compared to the world's average commuting time of 80 minutes.

Yet, road projects are every government's priority. Mumbai's coastal road, which will be used largely by the elite, has a budget of Rs 13,000 cr. The monorail is a white elephant which cost Rs 2,700 cr and incurs a loss of Rs 10 lakh a day.

Given Rs 15,000 cr the suburban railway can be overhauled, reducing the headway (frequency between trains on the same track) from four minutes to two, doubling the capacity of the suburban train network. Imagine how many cars this would take off the road. Instead, the thing on everyone's mind is the upcoming Metro network of 235 km at a cost of Rs 1,00,000 cr. It is slated to be fully functional by 2025 but will easily take until the end of the decade going by the way the plot for a key metro depot has become a political football.

Mumbai must also give serious thought to the bus rapid transport system (BRTS) which needs dedicated lanes for buses. Prime Minister Narendra Modi who made a success of the BRTS in Ahmedabad as the Gujarat CM is now fixated on the grandiose bullet train project. Talking about cycling and walkable footpaths invites strange looks.

On the other hand, populism has kept the suburban train fares ridiculously low with the minimum being Rs 5. In fact, the word *commuter* derives from reduced or commuted fare. In the mid-19th century America, the railways engendered suburbs in big cities and consequently daily travellers paying a reduced or 'commuted' fare.

Who would have dreamt that Mumbai's lifeline would come to such an abrupt and extended halt – since noon on March 22, to be precise. Mumbai's workforce is like an army of worker ants. The trains were full even when the city was flooded, even when there were communal riots or even when the Shiv Sena called a bandh. The world was stunned in 2006 when Mumbai's locals were packed as usual on July 12, the day after bombs planted by terrorists killed 207 commuters.

Mumbai's local trains are the stuff of Ripley's Believe It Or Not. If you sat in every local train for every journey, you would have made three rounds of the earth in a day!

The suburban network in Mumbai is an offshoot of the British-era railway meant to transport cotton from the hinterland to the ports and for fast movement of their troops. The first suburban train ran on 16th April 1853 between Bori Bunder, CSMT and Thane, a distance of 34 km.

One hundred and sixty-seven years later, suburban trains on the Central Railway, originating from CSMT, run 120 km up to Kasara, just 65 km short of Nashik and 113 km up to Khopoli, just 80 km short of Pune. On the Western Railway, they run 123 km from Churchgate to Dahanu, just 67 km short of Vapi in Gujarat. However, the attitude of the railway officials towards commuters retains the colonial aloofness. The railways consider it below its dignity to interact with state governments.

Another Ripley fact that has to be precisely measured is the overcrowding; experience suggests that it is eight to ten standing passengers per sq m but the oft-repeated figure is 14 to 16 per sq m. A nine-coach train is designed for a maximum of 1,500 passengers but carries 4,500 at peak time with ten to 12 hanging out of each door. Four of them fall off and die every day. Railway engineers who have had to reinforce the floor call it *Super-Dense Crush Load.*

Ironically, cattle are transported in greater comfort, being protected by the law. If Indian Railways carries more than 34 adult cows or buffaloes in a wagon, they can be prosecuted under the Prevention of Cruelty to Animals Act.

This writer can't forget the reaction of a Gujarati teenager waiting to board a local train at Sion station 15 years ago. It was a Sunday afternoon and there was just enough space in the compartment to stand without touching each other. As the train rolled into the station, the boy shouted excitedly out to his anxious parents, *"Khali chhe! Khali chhe!"* ('It's vacant! It's vacant!').

Strangely, this inhuman overcrowding doesn't find a mention in studies on commuting around the world, for example, in the IBM's oft-quoted 'global commuter pain' survey.

However, these hellish conditions don't seem to matter to our 'trained' commuters who have converted it into an extreme sport.

Boarding a local during 'crush' hour at the termini involves charging at an oncoming train while elbowing out fellow commuters and then timing the leap into the door to the nano-second, a superhuman feat that needs the guts of a gladiator and the grace of a gymnast. And what does the winner get — a window seat.

No wonder the chap falls asleep, having expended all his energy, mental and physical.

***

Walk the Talk on Footpaths

The conditions of pedestrians in Mumbai are comparable to those in England in the 19th century.

Sometimes politicians do talk about a worthwhile idea but it does not make news, partly because of their talk record and partly because the media fails to grasp the significance of the idea. This is how Aaditya Thackeray failed to hit the headlines despite promising to make major arterial roads in Mumbai pedestrian-friendly.

With glitzy metro lines, coastal roads and flyovers hogging attention, it is easy to forget that pedestrian trips account for a quarter to a third of all trips in Indian cities.

And despite the abysmal state of our footpaths – one of every ten traffic-related deaths in the country is a pedestrian — fatalism prevents us from demanding pedestrian rights.

Inaugurating the southbound arm of the new flyover at Kala Nagar last Sunday, Thackeray junior, minister for environment and tourism, had said that apart from arterial roads, pavements and pedestrian crossings too would be improved.

The problem is that pavements have never got the importance they deserve as we are obsessed with motorized transport. It is a shame that the British-built island city in Mumbai has proper footpaths but this can't be said of the suburbs which developed post-Independence.

It is another matter that the existing footpaths are uneven, full of obstructions and encroachment and at times even used by two-wheelers. We should be training our steeplechase athletes and motocross riders on the pavements of Mumbai.

Traffic police and municipal *chowkies* hog footpath space; the infamous Marine Drive rape happened in one such police post.

Here, hoardings are more important than avenue trees; a huge banyan tree was recently hacked at Girgaum Chowpatty in the heart of the city by hoarding firm contractors posing as civic employees.

We can only dream of the neat, tree-lined sidewalks in developed countries. According to Terence Bendixson, president of UK's Pedestrians Association for many years and author of 'Instead of cars', the conditions of pedestrians in Mumbai are comparable to those in England in the 19th century.

Believe it or not, there are guidelines for footpaths in India. Footpaths in residential areas need to be wide enough (1.8 m) for two wheelchairs to pass each other. In commercial zones, they have to be even wider, i.e. 2.5 m. Besides, the height of the kerb above the carriageway should not exceed 150 mm.

As for design, a footpath needs to be a flat walking surface (to prevent water stagnation), with guide tiles laid along its length to assist the visually impaired. Ideally, this walking zone should be clear of all obstructions including utility ducts, poles, electricity, water or telephone boxes, trees and signages.

Even the census brings out the primacy of the pedestrian. According to the 2011 national census, about 23% of work trips happen on foot, 13% on bicycle and 18% on public transport, with only 15% of trips on private transport.

Researchers say that the deaths of pedestrians in accidents is under-reported in India as they are not classified properly. Official statistics suggest that pedestrians comprise less than 10% of road accident deaths whereas the figure in third world countries is approximately 40% of traffic deaths.

According to a Union transport ministry report published in 2019, the average daily pedestrian fatalities in India went up from 34 in 2014 to 62 in 2018.

Significantly, pedestrian deaths rose by 84% between 2014 and 2018, says the report. A total of 12,330 pedestrians were killed across the country in 2014 and the number steadily rose to 22,656 in 2018.

West Bengal tops the list of pedestrian fatalities with 2,618 deaths from 2014 to 2018, followed by Maharashtra (2,515).

While 25% of the pedestrians killed on Maharashtra roads were in the 35-45 age group, 5% were under 18 years and 10% were senior citizens.

Mumbai traffic police records show that 447 people were killed in road mishaps in the city in 2019. According to the Bloomberg Philanthropies Initiative for Global Road Safety, 90% of these comprised pedestrians, cyclists and bikers.

'Super footpaths' were in the offing in Mumbai when the pandemic struck; the first of these was to be a six-metre-wide walkway from Siddhivinayak Metro station to Sewri via Prabhadevi and KEM hospital. No one's talking about it now, not even Aaditya Thackeray. In fact, the BMC budget for footpath repairs has been slashed by 86%.

Ironically, it was during the pandemic that the importance of footpaths was felt acutely. Hopefully, it will become an election issue too.

What better way to know a city than walking. Writer and journalist Khushwant Singh wrote about how he enjoyed his daily walk from his house in Colaba to his office at the *Illustrated Weekly* opposite what was then called the Victoria Terminus. Arun Sadhu, another writer-journalist, got to know Mumbai by tramping its streets.

Veteran journalist Vidyadhar Date, an ardent advocate of pedestrian rights and public transport and the author of '*Traffic in the era of climate change*', is carrying on in their tradition. He says that even in a city like Colombo one can walk for miles without ever getting off the footpath.

Indeed, there is no reason why Mumbai's footpaths cannot be of Colombo class when the BMC has set aside Rs 1,600 cr for improvement of roads even in this pandemic. And surely, the annual 'study trips' of our municipal corporators to Paris-London-Tokyo ought to result in some learning.

The handful of citizens' groups in Mumbai zealously guard their footpaths and want a 'footpath authority' that will give residents a greater say in maintaining their sidewalks.

The media too should wake up to the issue. Instead of merely running brand promotion campaigns such as *Happy Streets*, it must crusade for pedestrian rights.

To begin with, the media can ask Aaditya Thackeray to make the stretch from Bandra railway station to Kala Nagar, where he lives, pedestrian-friendly.

Politicians may promise us skywalks and the skies themselves but we must first make them walk the talk on footpaths.

Navi Mumbai, the Yardstick for Liveable Cities

Navi Mumbai is in a class of its own, being the largest planned city in India.

The difference hits you in the face as soon as you cross the Thane creek from Mumbai to Navi Mumbai; the narrow, clogged road widens into an eight-lane highway with flyovers at every junction, the in-your-face slums vanish, the railway stations are futuristic and the open spaces and greenery soothe the eyes.

If it were a beauty contest, Navi Mumbai would win it hands down on looks. Given its enviable quality of life, one can say that it would have aced the quiz round as well. Yet, when it comes to selecting India's most liveable cities, Navi Mumbai is vastly underrated.

This year, it ranks sixth in the list of liveable cities starting with Bengaluru, followed by Pune, Ahmedabad, Chennai and Surat. Those below Navi Mumbai in the top ten are Coimbatore, Vadodara, Indore and Greater Mumbai.

Actually, Navi Mumbai is in a class of its own, being the largest planned city in India. Flanked by the forested Parsik Hill range and an unbroken strip of mangroves, Navi Mumbai has vast open spaces, lagoons, gardens, tree cover and an excellent road and rail network. And the city's infrastructure is only set to improve in the next five years when the international airport coming up here is fully functional.

Last year Navi Mumbai was ranked as India's third-cleanest city. Now, it is striving to dislodge Indore from the top spot. As part of this effort, boundary walls are being painted in bright hues with slogans, social messages and various motifs on them.

Navi Mumbai is also one of the six cities — and the only one in Maharashtra — to receive a five-star rating in the list of garbage-free cities in a survey by the Ministry of Housing and Urban affairs.

The charm of Navi Mumbai is that it is half the size of Mumbai with just six per cent of its population. It occupies 344 sq km and has 1.3 million residents to Mumbai's 603 sq km and 20.4 million. And it is so close to Maximum City; the Thane creek which separates the two is just three km wide.

Navi Mumbai is the common man's city. Unlike Chandigarh, it is not a city for the affluent, a city for retired bureaucrats, landed gentry and businessmen. A 2010 survey by the City and Industrial Development Corporation (CIDCO) showed that the average family income in Navi Mumbai was Rs 25,000. The same survey revealed that 80% of the residents owned their houses.

Assured water supply, uninterrupted power, piped gas, footpaths and covered drains, reasonably good schools and colleges, neighbourhood shopping centres, malls, multiplexes and hospitals make it a liveable place.

Navi Mumbai though owes a debt to Chandigarh which came up in the fifties under the supervision of urban planner Le Corbusier. The conceptual design of Navi Mumbai was developed at the height of Modernism and features of this plan such as sector planning, hierarchy of roads and open spaces can be seen in Navi Mumbai.

The Union government's liveability survey — Ease of Living Index, 2020 – assessed 111 cities on four broad parameters — governance and social, physical and economic infrastructure. The index thus is an assessment tool that evaluates the quality of life and the impact of various initiatives for urban development. However, Navi Mumbai is about to turn 50 and thanks to the foresight of its planners it ticks all the boxes. Hence, other cities should be measured by the yardstick of Navi Mumbai.

Navi Mumbai is slightly below sea level and manages to keep out seawater through the Dutch design of holding ponds along the coast which hold the water during high tide. Over the years, beautiful gardens have come up around these ponds. At times, Punjabi films are shot here, passing off the holding ponds for Chandigarh's Sukhna lake.

According to Vandana Vasudevan, author of '*Urban Villager: Life in an Indian Satellite Town*', Navi Mumbai stands out as one of the most liveable satellite cities in the country with Greater Noida following at some distance.

The rest of the peri-urban towns, she says, have grown on steroids, prioritising swanky malls before drainage systems, rushing along haphazardly, blindly creating social and ecological imbalances. According to her, all of them struggle to define their identity and all have somehow fallen short of expectations, failing their stakeholders.

Going by Western standards though, Vienna, Melbourne and Sydney are the top three liveable cities while Damascus, Lagos and Dhaka rank at the bottom. New Delhi and Mumbai rank 118th and 119th out of 140 cities in the Economist Intelligence Unit's *Global Liveability Index 2019*.

Navi Mumbai has 175 civic gardens covering an area of 6.93 lakh sq m and a tree-to-human ratio of 1:2. It also has recreation centres for senior citizens. For youngsters, the Parsik hills provide an ideal trekking trail.

Navi Mumbai needs to curb pollution from the manufacturing hub of the Maharashtra Industrial Development Corporation (MIDC) and dust from illegal quarries and construction sites. As it is, its public hospitals are not in good shape. It also needs to add to its affordable housing stock.

The need of the hour though is to guard against unbridled redevelopment of aging housing colonies which threatens to ruin the character of the city. But so large and luscious is the redevelopment pie that it has brought big builders, unscrupulous politicians and corrupt officials to the same table.

Condominiums built three decades ago for the first settlers have been declared dilapidated and in imminent danger of collapse and the municipal corporation is in a hurry to evict the tenants without any transit camps, putting the onus on the builder.

Navi Mumbai is also repeating the other follies of Mumbai, such as constructing commercial complexes above bus depots and the slum rehabilitation scheme, with even lesser safeguards.

If this tendency to kill the golden goose is curbed, Navi Mumbai is about to get the one thing that it lacks, jobs. Among the big-ticket projects expected with the airport are the dedicated freight corridor to the nearby Jawaharlal Nehru port, the railway hub at Panvel, the 22-km trans-harbour link from Sewri in Mumbai to Nhava Sheva in Navi Mumbai, the Uran-Navi Mumbai rail link.

The liveability criteria ought to be redefined for cities such as Navi Mumbai which are spawning satellite cities of their own so that the very purpose of a planned city is not lost.

Section 6

Mumbai Undone

Open Spaces and Closed Minds

Deprived of open space, Mumbaikars feel uneasy if they can't locate another human at arm's length.

If there is one thing that defines Mumbai, it is density. Perhaps it is linked to its destiny; after all, this was an archipelago. The city that arose from the sea is still nibbling at it while gulping down mangroves, mudflats, creeks, and salt pans. Its roads swallow footpaths, towers swallow roads, so much so that we have to build a road in the sea.

The balconies, the open space in an apartment, have been swallowed by the drawing rooms. Mumbai's only open space is under flyovers because gardens and playgrounds have been swallowed on the drawing board itself. Having been deprived of open space for so long, Mumbaikars have adjusted to cramped places and feel uneasy if they can't locate another human at arm's length.

Instead of causing claustrophobia, it has had the opposite effect, agoraphobia. We are content with our per capita open space of 1.24 square metres. Our minister for environment and tourism Aaditya Thackeray has no idea of the blunder he has committed by promising to up that figure to 6 sq metres by 2040. He had better round it off to one square metre if his party hopes to retain power in the BMC. The city is about density.

The minister had better not mess with our minds. Earlier this month, all the municipal corporators were rushing to complete beautification projects in gardens and parks before their term ended as if their re-election depends on open spaces rather than on protecting the encroachment of open spaces by shopkeepers and slum dwellers.

The Thackeray scion is just a cub. He talks of increasing urban greenery when the BMC Act does not consider the maintenance of open spaces as a mandatory duty but mentions it as one of the civic body's several discretionary duties.

In 2017-18, the BMC allocated only 1.3 per cent of its total budget towards the maintenance of open spaces, reducing it to 0.7 per cent in the 2020-21 budget. Aaditya has been running around inaugurating a traffic island garden here, a seafront strip there, and posing on viewing decks by the sea.

Doesn't he know that the only tactical urbanism that Mumbai appreciates is vertical slums posing as skyscrapers, that the only view a Mumbaikar likes is that of his neighbour's apartment; it's a reality show which gives him insights into his own life. Sometimes though, he likes to see Hindi films because they show fantasies such as lovers running around trees. Since there's no space for planting trees in Mumbai, the government wants all new construction to have rooftop gardens.

And instead of planting trees in their plots, builders are told to maintain vertical gardens. They get away by naming their projects Green Acres, Eden Gardens, Whispering Palms, Nandanvan, Mahindra Gardens. The government bends over backward to tweak rules for the builders but none of the rules is about maintaining greenery in the housing complexes. Money doesn't grow on trees but the actions of the urban development department show that they believe that trees grow on money.

Mumbai is controlled by a real estate agenda that dictates arbitrary changes in land use and development control regulations. Hence it is that the contour maps showing flood-prone zones after the 2005 deluge were kept under wraps. There is a long history to this which stretches back more than a century.

The only time the city has thought of open spaces is at the time of pandemics. The 1898 plague led to a host of measures to improve sanitary and living conditions for which a development plan with 300 open spaces was drawn up. In the next pandemic, we may not have any space to build

Jumbo Covid centres, which will then be made on platforms anchored off the coast.

The World Health Organization (WHO) has set a minimum limit of nine square metres of open space per capita in urban areas, the UN has pegged this figure at 30 sq m, and the EU considers 26 sq m of open space per capita as acceptable. London has 31.68 sq m, New York City has 26.4 sq m and Tokyo has 3.96 sq m. In India, planning agencies follow the Housing Ministry's 2014 Urban and Regional Development Plan Formulation and Implementation guidelines, which suggest 10-12 sq m.

Delhi has 21.52 sq m, Bangalore has 17.32 sq m but Chennai has only 0.81 sq m. It can't be said that the BMC has not applied its mind to the problem. The 2014-34 development plan for Mumbai bumped up the percentage of open space in the city from 26 per cent in 2012 to 46 per cent in 2016 by changing the definition of open space.

Now, mangroves, mudflats, creeks, rivers, and even 'nullahs' – all of which are out of bounds — are counted as open spaces, putting Mumbai on par with Singapore and Sydney in terms of percentage of open space.

Ironically, these are the very spaces that architect P K Das, the man behind the Band Stand promenade, had suggested to be opened up to the public.

Instead of maintaining the land along the mangroves as an eco-sensitive border, he suggested integrating it in the urbanised area with the concept of promenades and cycling tracks and thus merging it with the idea of open spaces, to experience them as a part of the public realm. According to him, the idea of creating green spaces should not just be designated to the building of cute and fancy parks and gardens but for creating a network of open spaces, open and clear forever for all the citizens equally.

All this can happen only if the citizens demand it. Right now, Mumbaikars have a warped definition of open space. They are addicted to congestion. No one dare show them a dream about open spaces.

✳ ✳ ✳

The Gutter Politics That Mumbai Really Needs

The annual flooding of the city is treated as an act of God when it has got to do with a lack of action on gutters.

A one-minute clip of a bullock cart towing a car through a flooded Bombay street in 1932 – when Dadar and Bandra were at the edges of the city — went viral last week as the first monsoon showers submerged the city. Strangely, the BJP did not blame Nehru but the Shiv Sena, and for all the wrong reasons. Come to think of it, this is the time for gutter politics, literally.

Over the last 50 years, Mumbai's population has risen from 30 lakhs to two crores. Water supply has kept up, thanks to new dams more than 100 km away but not much brain has been expended on the drain.

The annual flooding is treated as an act of God. Not only was drainage ignored but slums and buildings came up in low-lying areas and even on reclaimed ponds and marshes to house the nearly seven-fold increase in population. The land area of the city has miraculously increased by almost 50 sq km in less than three decades since 1991.

The first reality check came on July 26, 2005 when more than 400 Mumbai residents perished in a deluge caused by the heaviest rainfall the city had witnessed in a century. That day, Mumbai received 944 mm of rain whereas the century-old storm-water drainage system of the city could cope with only 25 mm of rain a day. Who can forget the photograph of Shiv Sena leader Bal Thackeray being evacuated from his Kala Nagar bungalow in a boat when the Mithi river broke its banks.

Ever since, mini pumping stations and valves to prevent tidal water from entering the drains prevented flooding at Kala Nagar although it is a low-lying area, made worse by the elevated Bandra-Kurla Complex (BKC) next door. However, on June 9, the very first day of the monsoon, housing societies in Kala Nagar had knee-deep water in ground-floor flats. It turned out that the pumps were not working and the sea valves had not been closed.

As if this embarrassment was not enough, the widespread waterlogging in the city belied Mayor Kishori Pednekar's claim that "107 per cent of desilting work has been completed in all the drains in the city". And, as usual, the BMC and the Mumbai Metropolitan and Region Development Authority (MMRDA) passed the Kala Nagar buck to each other. This is the state of rain readiness in the CM's locality.

Another viral video showed two women falling, one by one, into an open manhole in a Mulund footpath. Since it was only waist deep, they were not swallowed like Dr Deepak Amrapurkar in August 2017, whose body was found days after the top gastroenterologist fell into an open manhole near Elphinstone Road railway station.

And would you believe it: The India Meteorological Department's Doppler radar – which warns us about cloud formation, rain and thunderstorms — is out of order and likely to remain defunct for at least the next two months. Also, no one knows what happened to all the rain gauges that were to be set up across the city.

How does all this square up with the fact that Mumbai is the second Indian city, after Chennai, to get its own integrated flood warning system, run by the BMC and the State Disaster Management Authority? CM Uddhav Thackeray had better ensure that such systems work if he wants to stay afloat in the Mumbai civic polls, less than a year away.

Every year, the BMC claims it is ready to tackle 350 to 450 mm of rain in a day but the existing drains are not ready even for 50 mm, while the pumping stations, crucial for preventing sea water from entering the drains during high tide and for pumping out storm water into the sea, often malfunction in the face of "more than heavy rainfall".

The Madhav Chitale committee that probed the 26/7 deluge recommended that Mumbai's rivers – there are four of them — and natural drains be widened and dredged, that encroachment on their banks be removed, that contour maps be made and flood-risk zones be demarcated and that construction in such zones be regulated, that new underground storm-water drains be laid with pumping stations, that mangroves be protected, that the municipal corporation be consulted before any construction in low-lying areas…

It was only after 26/7, as the Mumbai deluge of July 26, 2005 is known, that the BMC took up the Brimstowad project (Brihanmumbai Storm Water Disposal System), which was conceptualised in 1993 but rejected it for being too costly.

The Chitale committee had proposed setting up river development authorities for each of Mumbai's four rivers – Dahisar, Poisur, Oshiwara and Mithi — but it has been done only in the case of Mithi. Here too, the grand plans for river rejuvenation and beautification of the banks were reduced to pre-monsoon desilting.

While most of Chitale's recommendations were accepted, the one to demarcate flood-risk zones and to regulate construction in them remained on paper because of opposition from the builder lobby. Only half the projects initiated based on the committee's recommendations have been completed.

Meanwhile, 14 new flooding spots have emerged this year, taking the tally to 405, up from 386 last year and 273 the year before it.

Countries such as China are seeking to counter urban flooding through the concept of sponge cities which are structured to absorb and capture rainwater. In 2015, China selected 16 pilot sponge cities which had measures such as rooftop gardens, wetlands for rainwater storage and permeable pavements.

Mumbai instead, is eyeing one of the last open spaces left in the city, the salt pan lands. The MMRDA is looking at seven such plots totalling 300 acres between Kanjur Marg and Mulund for development. Now, these are the issues that the BJP ought to take up in their gutter politics.

The city's blind spot though is the threat of submergence by the sea which is rising at the rate of 1.7 mm per year along the Indian coast. Mumbai was marked as one of the coastal cities at risk of being submerged by 2050 in a study released in 2019 by Climate Central, a U S non-profit news organisation comprising scientists and journalists.

The news hit the front page but there has been hardly any discussion on it. What can one expect from Maharashtra which has no town planners in its urban development bodies and no hydrologists in its Water Resources Department.

However, there are still some scientists left in our scientific institutions and they say that the entire Mumbai will not be submerged by 2050 but there could be prolonged flooding in low-lying areas. After all, South Mumbai's Pydhonie (which translates as 'foot wash' in Marathi), was so named because the feet got wet in this stretch while crossing from one island to another at low tide.

Experts say it is time we create a 20-year climate change mitigation plan for Mumbai that will be linked to the city's development plan and civic budget. And that can happen only when voters tell the politicians that their bread and butter depends on the gutter.

Standing Committee or Understanding Committee?

The Brihanmumbai Municipal Corporation has been called the most corrupt organisation by none other than the Bombay High Court.

Former PM Morarji Desai is said to have described the notoriously corrupt Public Works Department or the PWD as Plunder Without Detection.

As far as the Brihanmumbai Municipal Corporation is concerned, no one has come close to Desai, even though the BMC has been labelled by none other than the Bombay High Court as the most corrupt organisation.

Wags have named it the Bombay Mining Company for its incessant, uncoordinated digging but that's like non-alcoholic beer. More about that later.

The same BMC did a sterling job of controlling COVID in Dharavi but the reason for harping on the money-guzzling *mahapalika* is that corruption seems to be finally becoming an issue in the forthcoming civic polls. Not because of a PIL or a journalistic expose or even a white paper by the Aam Aadmi Party.

The charges of big-time corruption in the richest civic body in India are being levelled by Shiv Sena's former ally, the BJP. The Shiv Sena, which has ruled BMC for the last two decades, has played the victim card. It may even work in the polls.

However, the charges are serious and the details are damaging. If the Income Tax Department is to be believed, Standing Committee Chairman Yashwant Jadhav and four contractors supposedly linked to him have 36 'benami' properties worth Rs 130 crore.

It also leaked to the media that a diary entry by Jadhav lists Rs 2 cr against 'Matoshree', which Jadhav says refers not to the residence of his party chief but his mother. Given that the BMC's budget for 2022-'23 is Rs 46,000 cr, this is a small change.

Anyway, diary entries have never amounted to much in court. What is known though is that the apex civic committee was famously described as the 'understanding committee' by former CM Vilasrao Deshmukh. The Sena seems to be on the back foot here.

Even small-time BJP leader Mohit Kamboj, whom the BMC was targeting, threatened to expose I S Chahal, the same officer who won accolades from WHO for his work in Dharavi. The CAG has questioned the BMC over a sharp increase in the construction cost of the Mumbai Coastal Road Project from Rs 252 crore in 2011 to Rs 1,274 crore in 2018 — a 405% rise. As of now, the estimated cost is 12,700 cr.

In the current civic budget, Rs 3,200 cr has been set aside for the 10-km-long stretch of the Coastal Road between the Princess Street Flyover and Worli. Just the cost of an international tourist centre in the 4.5-acre Worli Dairy plot is Rs 1,000 cr when the international cruise terminal at Indira docks is coming up at half the cost.

Even builders say that realty prices can be brought down by as much Rs 2,000 per sq ft if corruption is eliminated from the Buildings Proposal Department of the BMC.

Recently, four staffers in the BMC's Licence department were given executive postings even though they are facing bribery charges. Several black sheep were recalled in the name of staff shortage during COVID. The ideal plastic road project was reduced to a 100-metre patch in a remote corner of Bandra West and given a quiet burial. A company that was blacklisted in Pune was within a fortnight given works worth Rs 100 crore for five COVID centres in Mumbai.

The three companies hired for medical oxygen supply were blacklisted and two of them failed to deliver but were not penalised. While the average cost across in India for a sewage treatment plant is Rs 1.7 crore per million litre, BMC floated the tender at Rs 7.47 crore per million litre.

The Supreme Court is now monitoring the process. It is unfair to single out the BMC though. Urban local bodies across the country are notoriously inefficient even in corruption.

For the common man, the municipality is the *ulti-palty* but wags have done no justice to it. Recently, an audit into the South Delhi Municipal Corporation revealed "irregularities of over Rs 1,600 crore". This is when Delhi's municipalities have failed to pay teachers and sanitation workers' salaries on time. We simply seem to have accepted widespread corruption in our civic bodies.

What can the poor citizen do if he can't get the body of a relative killed in an accident without bribing the morgue clerk? Here are some more news items buried in the inside pages: The Bombay HC ordered CIDCO, MMRDA, the Vasai-Virar Municipal Corporation to file affidavits by February 21 about allegations in a PIL that the development plan for the area was in limbo for 13 years, during which 883 reserved plots were encroached upon and funds misused.

The Mithi River Project in Mumbai, which includes dredging, constructing a security wall and service road, is incomplete even after 17 years, during which Rs 1,150 cr has been spent on it. In Paithan, an RTI query revealed that civic works for Rs 80,000 were billed at Rs 8 lakhs by the surreptitious addition of a zero.

Urban planners say that civic bodies in India suffer from either understaffing, which leads to a failure to deliver basic urban services, or overstaffing of untrained manpower, a shortage of qualified technical staff, and managerial supervisors.

Lack of supervision has resulted in an unwillingness to innovate methods for service delivery. It is time to ask some tough questions about the quality of governance in urban local bodies. Are the taxes we pay being put to good use? Are infrastructure projects chosen based on what's best for the public or best for the ruling party?

What is the benchmark for civic services? What is the accountability of civic officials? And lastly, are our municipal corporations working to a plan?

In this context, it is heartening to see Mohalla Committee members in Pune urge citizens to join them on a one-day inspection tour of their localities before they cast their votes in the upcoming civic polls.

Finally, here are two weak attempts at matching Morarji Desai: Best Method of Corruption and Bombay's Mindboggling Corruption.

Our Fire Plan Has Gone Up in Smoke

Let alone learn from the Uphaar cinema hall fire 25 years ago, we have not made even our hospitals safe.

Nero fiddled while Rome burnt. Our *'netas'* are no better. As high-rise after high-rise and hospital after hospital go up in flames, they are busy blowing their own trumpets, trombones, and *'tutaris'*.

In Maharashtra, a fire in the very seat of power, Mantralaya, failed to jolt three consecutive CMs into action. Ten years after the inferno that gutted four floors of the secretariat, killing five people, the state is still unprepared. Pulled up by the Bombay High Court on Monday for having "wholly failed" to justify its "complete inaction" over fire safety draft rules framed in 2008, the state came up with a ludicrous explanation

In a reply that makes Nero look naive, the state government came up with this classic. It said that the 2012 fire at Mantralaya had destroyed the files and rendered a follow-up on the draft regulation difficult; a tacit admission that Maharashtra's fire plan had literally gone up in smoke! The court retorted that notwithstanding the fire, the state didn't find it difficult to come up with the 2034 Development Plan. Adding to the embarrassment, it came on the eve of the National Fire Service Week, April 14 to April 20.

As it is, India has the dubious distinction of logging every fifth fire-related death in the world. This came out in a 195-nation analysis by Global Diseases Burden published in the BMJ Injury Prevention journal. It said that

India recorded 27,027 of the 1.2 lakh fire-related deaths reported globally in 2017. The National Crime Records Bureau, which compiles all deaths due to accidents, presents a less alarming picture. According to it, fire accounted for 2.6 per cent of all accident-related deaths in 2019. A total of 10,915 people died in fires that year in 11,037 incidents, 58 per cent of which were in homes.

Fire safety in homes has figured recently in the Supreme Court as well. In 2018, the apex court sought a response from all state governments on a PIL alleging a flagrant violation of fire safety norms specified in the National Building Code-2016 by builders. The petitioner, a non-government organisation called United Human Rights Federation, had also alleged that there appeared to be a collusion between authorities and developers in the grant of fire safety clearance. These mild queries don't amount to much. However, a rare judgment in such cases is the one regarding the 40-storey Supertech twin towers in NOIDA that are to be demolished next month. Again, going by 'concrete' evidence, this 'trial by ire' has limited utility.

In Monday's dressing down, the Bombay HC too had harped on the need to include special provisions relating to fire safety under the National Building Code (NBC) in Maharashtra's Development Control Rules. The NBC stipulates a slew of safety measures such as high-speed lifts with backup power supply in skyscrapers exclusively for firemen. The NBC specifies how many exits should be provided in a particular kind of building and where they must be placed. Twenty-five years ago, 59 people died of suffocation in the Uphaar Cinema hall fire in Delhi because the escape routes had been blocked.

Let alone learn from this, we have not made even our hospitals safe. Last year, Maharashtra witnessed six hospital fires in which 55 perished, including newborns and COVID patients. Admonishing the state government, the HC had said that it did not want hospitals turning into potential "Jatugrih/ Lakshagrih" — a house made of wax through which the Kauravas attempted to eliminate the Pandavas during their exile.

The first stage towards a fire-safe building is to use fire-resistant/ retardant materials and install smoke detection/fire alarm systems. In the fire at Tardeo's 20-storey Sachinam Heights, where nine perished in January, the lid of the electrical junction box where the fire originated was not fire-resistant. The firefighting system of the building itself was out of order. For that matter, neither the sprinklers nor the fire hydrants at Mantralaya worked in 2012.

The NBC makes fire compartmentalisation (area/floor wise) mandatory to restrict the spread of fire through horizontal and vertical spaces. A fire on the 12th floor of the 26-storey Mont Blanc building at Kemps Corner in December 2013 was restricted to the same floor, thanks to the proper insulation of the utility ducts which otherwise would carry hot air upwards, causing a flash fire in the higher floors. Yet, seven people died in the incident; two from burns and five from suffocation.

A key requirement in a building over 30 metres high is an underground water tank and an overhead water tank connected by a pipe that runs through the building (wet riser) and has hose pipes on each floor. However, in most fires, it is found to be unusable because of a lack of maintenance. According to the Mumbai fire brigade, of the 324 fires reported in the city's high-rises between January 2020 and October 2021, as many as 127 buildings did not have an operational fire fighting system. When the internal fire-fighting mechanism in high-rises fails, firemen have to lug 150 kg pumps and install them on every tenth floor to train water jets at the fire.

The use of modern technology can go a long way in managing fire risks. Artificial Intelligence has been used in risk assessment. IoT and Blockchain are used to automatically send alerts when risks are detected. However, most people who live in high-rise flats worth crores loathe spending on basic fire-fighting gadgets. Awareness of fire safety is abysmal in India. Textbooks should have a chapter on it and students should be put through regular fire drills.

Everyone should remember that safety is a choice, not a chance.

✳ ✳ ✳

Section 7

Mumbai: Flora and Fauna

Wetlands Are Not Wastelands

Wetlands create habitats for aquatic plants and are vital for flood control.

The World Wetlands Day on February 2 went unnoticed in Mumbai; seven islands that swallowed the sea and are still gobbling up creeks, mangroves, marshes, lakes, saltpan lands, rivers and even drains.

The city of gold is unaware of its natural wealth. It can see the pot of gold at the end of the rainbow but fails to see the link between its vanishing wetlands and the heat and dust that are choking its residents. The lust for lucre has blinded the commercial capital of India to the fact that these wetlands are not only the city's lungs and a nursery for marine life but also its first line of defence against rising sea levels, tidal waves, floods and erosion.

Mumbai has a Climate Action Plan but just outside the city limits, the land sharks, the sand mafia and even corporates and municipal corporations have their own plans. The high court has to remind them of the law of the land. Garbage and debris are merrily dumped in mangroves. Forest status has been granted to mangroves but no government body wants to transfer the land to the forest department.

When it suits the authorities, Powai Lake falls off the national wetland atlas. When it suits the planners, a feeding site for flamingos mapped by the late ornithologist Salim Ali becomes a fit place for a golf course and a housing complex. And why shouldn't they think so? The Bandra-Kurla

Complex, the financial nerve centre of the country, and Malad's MindSpace, a mini-BKC, are nothing but reclaimed mangrove land.

The Flamingo habitat at Seawoods, Navi Mumbai, a wetland that local residents Shruti and Sunil Agarwal have been trying to save from land sharks as well as the City and Industrial Development Corporation.

Credit: Surabhi Agarwal

When will it occur to us that wetlands are not shallow water bodies with no utility but ecosystems as important as forests? When will it dawn on us that wetlands are biodiversity hotspots? Wetlands are areas permanently or seasonally saturated in water, which create habitats for aquatic plants and are vital for flood control, as they absorb excess flow from rain, while recharging groundwater.

The United Nations says that due to a lack of effective management mechanisms and proper appreciation of their true worth, nearly 90 per cent of the world's wetlands have been degraded since the 1700s and we are losing wetlands three times faster than forests. In February last year, the state environment department had submitted to the Bombay High Court that the number of wetlands in Maharashtra had shrunk from 44,714 in 2010, to 15,865 in 2020, on account of a change in the definition of wetlands in the Union Environment ministry's 2017 Wetland Rules.

If one looks at Mumbai from the air, the huge creeks with their mangrove belts are the most distinguishable features. Creeks account for almost 12 per cent of the area of Mumbai; 71 sq km out of 604 sq km. In fact, the size of the island city – Colaba to Mahim – is just 68 sq km. Thane creek which separates Navi Mumbai from Mumbai is one of the largest creeks in Asia. Vasai, Malad, Gorai, Mahim and Mahul are the other creeks but since Mumbai lacks water transport, no one realises that the true open spaces of the city are the creeks. This is the case of Navi Mumbai as well, which is sandwiched between the Panvel and the Thane creeks. It has an unbroken garland of mangroves which will be history before the city turns 100. Also history will be the flamingos that flock in thousands to the mud flats in this city. As it is, studies show that Mumbai has lost 40 per cent of its mangrove cover in the last two decades.

Architect and housing activist P K Das, the man behind the Band Stand and Carter Road promenades, has been saying for ten years that Mumbai must re-imagine its open spaces and include wetlands in them. Instead of maintaining the land along the mangroves as an eco-sensitive border, he suggests integrating it in the urbanised area with the concept of promenades and cycling tracks. "This will also contribute to enormous recreational activity as citizens can walk, cycle along the marshy bushes and also learn about the ecosystem," he argues.

Going by the Maharashtra forest department, the Mumbai Metropolitan region, which extends to Matheran in the West and Palghar in the north, has six wetlands. The Thane creek flamingo sanctuary (TCFS) management plan 2020-2030, has officially designated six sites – Bhandup (11 ha) in Mumbai, Panje (124 ha), Belpada (30 ha), Bhendkhal (8 ha) in Uran, Training Ship Chanakya (13 ha), NRI Complex (19 ha) in Navi Mumbai – as wetlands. The identification of these six sites as wetlands was done based on a report by the Bombay Natural History Society (BNHS).

As for Ramsar sites – internationally recognised wetlands – Maharashtra has two of them: the Nandur Madhameshwar wetland near

Nashik and the Lonar lake in Buldana. The former has been formed by shallow backwaters of the Nandur Madhmeshwar dam but the tourist facilities there are rudimentary. Lonar Lake was created by a meteorite collision impact during the Pleistocene Epoch. It is one of the four known, hyper-velocity, impact craters in basaltic rock anywhere on Earth; the other three are in southern Brazil. India has 49 Ramsar sites, the prominent ones being Chilika in Orissa, Sunderbans in West Bengal, Vembanad in Kerala and Kolleru in Andhra Pradesh. The proposal to tag the Thane creek as a Ramsar site is pending.

In Mumbai and its vicinity, it is the citizens who are at the forefront of the fight to save wetlands. Shruti and Sunil Agarwal are known as the saviours of flamingos in Navi Mumbai but their activism started with a simple police complaint in 2016 about the destruction of mangroves near their house in Seawoods. They have been fighting to save the 80 hectares of wetlands abutting their colony that are home to thousands of flamingos. The CIDCO wants to convert this wetland into a golf course and residential complex. B N Kumar, a media professional and Nandkumar Pawar, a fisherman, teamed up with Uran villagers and thanks to their relentless media campaign, the Uran municipal council was forced to stop dumping in the mangroves. They have also documented the destruction of the Panje wetland, saving it in the nick of time.

Jyoti Nadkarni and Nareshchandra Singh got together a band of like-minded people to save the Kharghar wetlands in Navi Mumbai from being overrun by brick kilns, shrimp farmers and slums. Dharmesh Barai and his group of volunteers spend each weekend cleaning the mangroves and lakes of litter. Not to mention stalwarts such as Debi Goenka, Stalin Dayanand, Sumaira Abdulali, Bittu Sehgal and others.

Sustained pressure by the greens led the state wetland authority, chaired by cabinet minister Aaditya Thackeray, to direct all district collectors to submit a fresh assessment of wetlands in their jurisdiction.

✳ ✳ ✳

Missing the Wood for the Trees

Despite all the homilies we have yet to formulate an urban tree policy.

At the beginning of every year Mumbai goes gaga over the magical rosy hue along the Eastern Express highway at Vikhroli, thanks to a row of Pink Trumpet trees.

When the bloom ends, so does the euphoria and any interest it has evoked in flowering trees or for that matter, in trees themselves. As a result, it has gone unnoticed that Mumbai is facing a biodiversity crisis because of its choice of avenue trees.

When the city was expanding rapidly in the eighties, the BMC opted for the non-native Peltophorum, the Gulmohur and the Rain tree over native Indian flowering trees because they grow fast and their saplings have a good survival rate.

The Peltophorum from Southeast Asia with its golden yellow flowers and the flaming red Gulmohur from Madagascar do add a splash of colour in the summer with the Rain tree, native to South America, providing a canopy but for the rest of the year the first two are positively ugly. In fact, the preponderance of these trees gives the city the drab look of industrial greenery.

People have even forgotten what other flowering trees look like. How many, for instance, can identify the Pride-of-India (Lagerstroemia speciosa), Palash (Butea monosperma), also known as Flame of the forest, the evergreen

Bakul (Mimusops elengi) with fragrant flowers and the Karanj (Millettia pinnata) with its small white and purple flowers.

The delicate violet flower of the Pride-of-India ('Tamhan' in Marathi) is the state flower of Maharashtra but how many Tamhan trees do you see at Mantralaya or at the Vidhan Sabha or even in parks and in posh housing complexes?

All this, coupled with our own disconnect with nature, has subconsciously led us to devalue trees and think of them as disposable *'jhaad-jhankaad'*. Housing societies don't think twice before hacking trees because bird droppings mess up cars or because people have an irrational fear of bats, which sometimes roost in the bigger trees.

If there is a tree blocking a hoarding it is sure to be axed or poisoned, as was the case with an entire row of Rain trees lining the road to Vashi railway station. In the nineties, a hoarding firm in Mumbai even got a court order restraining the growth of a tree in Prabhadevi.

Even civic authorities have become so callous that some years ago, a tree-lover in Navi Mumbai had to get a court order to uproot paver blocks suffocating the stems of avenue trees.

A decade and half ago the Shiv Sena, which rules the BMC, proposed the hacking of several century-old trees in the Byculla zoo to build a viewing gallery-cum-cafeteria. Mercifully, the proposal was dropped.

Three years ago, landmark trees in South Mumbai were hacked and pulled out in a shamefully primitive way for the new-age transport solution, the Metro. And the cynical ploy to cut more than 2,000 fully-grown trees overnight at the Aarey mini forest for a Metro car shed is now a deplorable chapter in the city's history.

Who can then force builders to retain or transplant trees although they sell their concrete creations as Whispering Palms, Nilgiri Gardens, Gulmohar Park, Edenwoods, Meadows…

Lanes and localities named after native trees still exist in Mumbai but the trees themselves have vanished.

And where is the effort by the BMC to create distinctive avenues with Indian flowering trees? Dr Ashok Kothari of the Bombay Natural History

Society (BNHS) who has created a Bakul avenue at SNDT Women's University at Santa Cruz, says there was a time when the first thing Britishers did on disembarking was to go on a tree tour of Mumbai in an open buggy.

Where is the effort to institute Best Tree/Avenue awards in every ward? With tree tax adding to its humongous budget, why can't Mumbai get a specialized machine to excavate trees for transplantation with their main root intact? Why can't the richest municipal corporation in India get jet sprays to clean the trees of dust and grime?

Coming back to non-native or exotic trees versus native Indian trees, arborist Avinash Kubal, says, "Today, the exotic trees outnumber the native ones and this is leading to a serious ecological imbalance."

Marselin Almeida and Naresh Chaturvedi, co-authors of *The Trees of Mumbai*, published by the BNHS, point out that exotic species planted for ornamental purposes account for half of Mumbai's tree diversity of 318 species. The latest tree census puts the figure at 52 per cent.

Unlike trees native to the Indian sub-continent which have adapted to our climatic conditions over millions of years, the exotic species being used as ornamental avenue trees are not native to India. Most of them have shallow roots and topple easily in a storm, they are also susceptible to diseases.

What is more significant is that exotic trees don't produce any fruits that birds or insects can eat and their branch structure is unsuitable for nesting.

On the other hand, indigenous trees are a source of food and shelter for birds, animals and insects. "Imagine the biodiversity Mumbai is losing because these non-native trees form half its tree cover," says Kubal who insists that it is high time we start recognizing them as invasive species and replacing them with native Indian trees.

Many Western countries have banned non-native species. The US does not allow even Indian Tulsi (holy basil) to be grown in their country.

Of late, Mumbai has stopped planting exotic trees but civic bodies in Mumbai's satellite townships are still promoting them. However, experts say there's no harm in planting a few exotic trees; the Pink Trumpet tree (Tabebuia rosea) itself is one.

Mumbai has 2.9 million trees according to the latest civic survey of 2018, a figure that activists say is vastly inflated as the previous one in 2008 showed two million trees. The greenest suburb is Ghatkopar with 2.92 lakh trees while Masjid-Dongri figures at the bottom with 7,816.

The BMC's Environment Status Report, 2017-18, shows that the city has one tree for every four people, way short of the eight trees per person recommended by a study of the Indian Institute of Science (IISc), Bengaluru.

The fact is that despite all the homilies we have yet to formulate an urban tree policy or an urban green space policy. This is the reason why metros in developing countries have less than five per cent tree cover as compared to 20 per cent in Western countries.

That brings us to what we started out with. Unless Mumbai has beautiful avenue trees such the Pink Trumpet or Pride-of-India, citizens will not fall in love with trees. Instead, trees will keep falling on them.

Handy Facts About the Bird in the Bush

Some 200 avian species can be seen in each of our four metros despite the concrete jungles they are.

It took the disappearance of the sparrow – Passer domesticus – to kindle interest in birds. There are hundreds of bird-watching clubs and annual events where thousands compete to record avian species in their backyards. Even congested cities like Mumbai have bird sanctuaries. Today happens to be World Migratory Bird Day, a UN-backed campaign dedicated to raising awareness about migratory birds and the need for international cooperation to conserve them. And yes, there's a World Sparrow Day too, on March 20.

The lockdown helped increase the population of sparrows and bird watchers also spotted species normally not seen in cities. There are some 9,700 species of birds, of which around 1,350 are found in India; 81 of them are endemic to the Indian subcontinent. Surprisingly, some 200 species can be seen in each of our four metropolitan cities.

So, why don't we see them? Questions like this show who really is bird-brained. We don't see birds simply because we have destroyed their habitat. There's hardly any foliage, open space, wetlands or water bodies. Worse, housing societies cement their compounds to use every inch for parking and modern architecture leaves no nooks and niches for birds. And it is only now that we are realising that exotic trees such as Peltophorum, Gulmohar and the raintree, which heavily outnumber the native Indian trees, don't support avian life as they don't produce any fruits that birds or insects can eat and their branch structure is unsuitable for nesting.

Now, how many have seen the native Palash tree with its bright orange-red flowers that are regularly visited by birds for nectar? No wonder we are left with scavengers such as crows and pigeons. Incidentally, the yellow-footed green pigeon (Hariyal in Marathi) is the state bird of Maharashtra. Unlike its city cousin, the rock pigeon, it's a shy bird which prefers wooded habitats and lives on fruits.

This doesn't mean that one has no chance of sighting a bird in the concrete jungle. Those who live near a creek or a forested patch, a housing complex with native trees and a garden can spot several birds from their windows. And those with terrace or balcony gardens are rewarded with daily visits of the shiny sunbird, a flying jewel.

Wildlife photographer and conservationist Sunjoy Monga has spotted a dozen species from his Lokhandwala flat; the red-vented bulbul, the red-whiskered bulbul, the oriental magpie-robin, the common tailor bird, the Asian koel, the white-spotted fantail, the purple-rumped sunbird, the rose-ringed parakeet, the Alexandrine parakeet, the Eurasian golden oriole, the white-throated kingfisher and the coppersmith barbet.

The last-named is the official bird of Mumbai. The tiny coppersmith barbet is green with a red head, yellow cheeks and a yellow throat. Its characteristic call – tuk, tuk, tuk – sounds like a coppersmith striking metal with a hammer. The bird carves out holes inside a tree to build its nest and is predominantly fruit-eating, though it has also been observed eating insects.

Vile Parle housewife Madhuri Deshmukh photographed some 25 species of birds during the lockdown from her seventh-floor window which looks down on a giant peepal tree. She's also part of a team that has compiled a three-minute audio-visual on birds that can be seen in Mumbai's residential areas. The AV features images and calls of 19 birds and it's a delight to hear the sharp cry of the Indian golden oriole, the persistent harp of the common tailorbird and the passionate song of the oriental magpie robin. However, words, even AVs, fail to capture the beauty of a bird and the thrill of spotting it in nature.

If one looks carefully, one can find birds even in open fields. The desert wheatear, the common stonechat, a migrant from Central Asia, the long-tailed shrike and wagtails have been spotted at the Mahalaxmi racecourse in Mumbai.

The mangroves and wetlands along the coast of Mumbai and of neighbouring Thane and Navi Mumbai are the best sites for birding apart from the national park. At one such spot, the Lokhandwala lake, Monga recorded 122 species, including migratory birds such as the northern pintails which fly all the way from Europe.

Talking of migratory birds, the Arctic tern holds the long-distance migration record for birds, flying between Arctic breeding grounds and the Antarctic each year. Great snipes, small stocky birds that wade in the marshes, make non-stop flights of 4,000–7,000 km, lasting 60 to 90 hours. Some bar-tailed godwits, a large wader that feeds on bristle-worms and shellfish on coastal mudflats and estuaries, have the longest known non-stop flight of any migrant, flying 11,000 km from Alaska to New Zealand.

Around 50 million birds migrate every year. India falls under the Central Asian Flyway for the north-south winter migration. If Salim Ali, the Birdman of India, were alive today, he would have been happy to see that India has launched a national action plan to protect 29 wetlands frequented by migratory birds. He would have been saddened, though, to see the destruction of wetlands and mangroves in the Uran-Ulwe belt in Navi Mumbai, one of his favorite birding spots.

Gulls, terns, shorebirds and flamingoes ringed in Central Asia, Persian Gulf, Eastern Asia and the Indian Ocean islands have been recorded on Maharashtra's coast. Flamingoes, most of which come from Kutch in Gujarat, are the biggest draw in Mumbai. They migrate mainly at night and can travel 600 km in one night.

There are 15 Indian birds on the critically endangered list, headed by the Great Indian Bustard. Weighing up to 15 kg and growing up to one metre in height, it's one of the heaviest flying birds. Less than 200 of them are left now, of which about 100 are in Rajasthan.

As for the most beautiful bird of India, it's undoubtedly the rarely seen Himalayan Monal. It resembles a peacock, but is much smaller and has distinguishing features such as an iridescent rainbow-like plumage, a wiry metallic head and crest, and a reddish-brown neck. The satyr tragopan or the crimson-horned pheasant, again a Himalayan bird, and the Asian paradise flycatcher with its amazingly long tail are the other eye-catchers.

We need birds more than they need us. They are such efficient pest-eaters that nest boxes have become a pest control practice throughout Europe. Birds spread seeds and hummingbirds and honeyeaters help in pollination. Vultures act as scavengers and curb disease. Birds respond quickly to changes in the environment and are our early warning system for climate change, biodiversity loss and pollution. As Amy Fraenkel, Executive Secretary of the Convention on the Conservation of Migratory Species of Wild Animals, says in her message for World Migratory Bird Day: "The journey of a migratory bird knows no borders and therefore, neither should our response to the planetary crisis."

As for us, we should apply the green mantra, 'Think global, act local'. It's time we start creating bird parks just as we have butterfly gardens. Come to think of it, a bird in the bush is worth its weight in gold for a generation that hasn't seen a sparrow.

Encourage Footfalls at Waterfalls

Rape the Western Ghats but don't let city folks enjoy the waterfalls in them.

Splashing about in a forest pond, enjoying a Jacuzzi in a swirling rivulet or simply soaking in the spray of a waterfall while the greenery and the mist play hide and seek… Sadly, rejuvenation in the rains has been ruled out this year, not really because of the pandemic but because the authorities don't want any drowning cases. In fact, several waterfalls and lakes around Mumbai have been out of bounds for a couple of years for this reason.

On June 8, the collector of Thane district, which has all the picnic spots around Mumbai, banned gatherings near waterfalls, lakes and dams to "prevent accidents at water bodies in the region". The order has been issued under Section 144 of the Code of Criminal Procedure, the Epidemic Diseases Act and the Disaster Management Act, laws that should have been invoked for the Haridwar Kumbh.

Last weekend, motorists from Mumbai headed for the popular Bhushi dam in Lonavala were turned back from the hill station. Half of them wouldn't have driven all the way uphill had they been allowed access to Pandavkada at Kharghar. Here, water plunges from a height of 107 metres, forming a milky column 34 metres taller than the Kutub Minar. The Navi Mumbai police have prohibited entry to it, terming it a dangerous place as two revellers drowned and two others were washed away in a downpour in 2019.

Pandavkada waterfalls, which drain into a vast empty plain, can easily be developed into a tourist attraction on the lines of the Jog falls (253m) in Karnataka or the Dudhsagar falls (310m) on the Goa-Karnataka border. The tallest plunge waterfall in India though, is the Nohkalikai falls (340m) near Cherrapunji in Meghalaya.

The scenic Malshej Ghat, on the border of Thane and Pune districts, with its numerous waterfalls is also out of bounds.

But such is the lure of pristine nature that people sneak into such spots. Earlier this week, four youngsters drowned in two days at Nilapani Lake in the Yeoor range of the Sanjay Gandhi National Park in Thane. Inviting forest pools sometimes have weeds, in which the legs get entangled. The local police have now written to the forest department, seeking measures to stop people from entering the lake.

Surely, there is something wrong with this approach; this is throwing the baby out with the bath water. Do we stop travelling by local trains in Mumbai although we know that four commuters fall off and die every day? Do we stop using two-wheelers in the monsoon just because flooded potholes trip up some riders? Do we stop vaccination for fear of an adverse reaction? The remedy is to forewarn revellers of the dangers, make the place safer by putting up warning boards/maps and to deploy guides/lifeguards.

Blanket bans such as these are also bound to affect trekkers to the cloud-draped forts, foggy pinnacles, temples and Buddhist caves that dot the Sahyadris. In fact, the Thane collector's order does ban assemblies at Siddhagad hills, Harishchandragad fort, as well as at Barvi and Padale dams.

Where should Mumbaiites who have just 1.24 sq m of accessible open space per person go to recharge themselves? Deprived of playgrounds and gardens, they are being denied nature's gifts.

Monsoon treks are the only time city folks have a communion with nature. With a little bit of effort — scout camps, school/college trips led by botanists — they can be introduced to the unique flora and fauna of the region. The Bombay Natural History Society does an admirable job of it.

The Western Ghats – a World Natural Heritage hotspot – are an enchanted forest in the rains, with the pink flowers of the wild turmeric, lilies, orchids, flowers that stink of rotting flesh, ant hills, giant spiders, huge moths, butterflies, land crabs, tree frogs… Can all this be seen at a manicured water park?

The irony is that while entry to waterfalls is banned, illegal quarrying, open-cast mines, sand dredging, hooch stills, poaching and encroachment are in full swing. Rape the Western Ghats but don't let city folks enjoy the waterfalls. The Western Ghats have an estimated 5,000 species of flowering plants, 139 mammal species, 508 bird species and 325 globally endangered species.

Five years ago, Sanjay Bhatia, then MD of CIDCO, told this correspondent that Pandavkada waterfalls would reopen in a year after being spruced up. It remains closed and blasts at an illegal quarry next door shake Kharghar buildings half-a-kilometre away. Talk of smart cities.

Popular waterfalls, lakes, river rafting, forest trails, mountain treks etc should be brought under the purview of the tourism department, which will then liaise with the forest and the meteorological departments and the police. For weekend getaways such as Bhushi dam and Karjat's Bhivpuri Falls, thronged by nearly 10,000 revellers during weekends, an e-pass could be introduced to regulate the numbers.

Regular weather updates and basic safety tips can be put up on the official website, local youth trained as guides/lifeguards and guards stationed at entry points to prevent revellers from carrying liquor or plastic into the forest. A nominal fee can be charged for entry and for services such as parking, restrooms, changing rooms and first aid. The locals can also benefit by putting up eateries and selling local forest produce. Is this too difficult? Himachal Pradesh has been doing it since ages.

A media campaign is needed but leading newspapers are busy with marketing gimmicks such as Happy Streets. The greens too restrict themselves to their narrow agendas. The job of rooting for waterfall tourism is left to enthusiasts such as Dharmesh Barai, whose group picks up the trash at the site.

PM Modi spoke about employment generation through local tourism but governments still need to be prodded by the courts. Lifeguards were deployed at Mumbai's beaches in 2006 only after a high court order. In Goa, the 700 lifeguards and beach marshals of Drishti Lifesaving hired by the tourism department since 2008 have led to a 99 per cent reduction in deaths due to drowning and significantly improved the tourist experience in Goa.

How many lives will be lost before Maharashtra realises that footfalls at waterfalls mean more than those at water parks?

Section 8

Contempt for Citizens

Civil Servants: Caretakers or Undertakers?

Are our civil servants running the country or ruining the country?

Every year we cheer as the best and the brightest youngsters are selected for the civil services, a job that requires them to virtually run the country. Not for nothing is it said that the three engines of India's governance are the DM (district magistrate), the CM and the PM. So, how is it that these IAS and IPS officers, the 24-carat gold of our country, get involved in something as revolting as the cover-up the Dalit girl's rape and murder in Hathras, the DM in this case even disgracing himself on national TV by threatening the family of the victim?

How do the chief secretary and the director-general of police of UP justify something as outrageous as cremating the rape victim in the dead of night while keeping her family confined to their house? All this in full media glare. Have our caretakers have turned into our undertakers?

The Hathras episode which comes on the heels of the Unnao rape case, where the victim tried to set herself on fire outside CM Yogi Adityanath's house to draw attention to her plight, is yet another instance of the complicity of civil servants in patently illegal acts.

Given political will, our babus can work wonders such as containing COVID in the sprawling Dharavi slum through innovative social distancing measures.

Credit: Prashant Nakwe

Then, who can forget the UP government's move to name and shame anti-CAA protestors while gangsters such as Vikas Dubey were being wooed. Also fresh in memory is the midnight lathi-charge on sleeping supporters of Baba Ramdev at Delhi's Ramlila Maidan in 2012 which resulted in a stampede leading to a woman's death. The classic case though remains 'nasbandi', the forcible sterilization drive during the Emergency.

Forget the big moments, our bureaucrats can't stop corruption in midday meal schemes for poor children, and they can't ensure that orphans in shelter homes are not raped, they can't implement even dog sterilization projects. All they can do is lock up one actress on drug charges while providing 'Y' security to another actress.

Why do we expect them to nab the killers of Dabholkar, Pansare, Kalburgi and Gauri Lankesh when they are busy arresting renowned professors and scholars under anti-terrorist laws? How do we expect them to curb crimes against women when the cop in charge of law and order in UP displays his ignorance of the post-Nirbhaya definition of rape on prime time while trying to deny that the Hathras girl was raped. Has he been promised the same carrot, a party ticket, as the Bihar Director-General of Police (DGP) who raked up the Sushant Singh Rajput case?

Why do we expect bureaucrats to do anything about local goons, illegal quarrying or encroachment of mangroves, forests or salt pans by land sharks or to take steps to curb air pollution? Don't we know that IAS stands for I Am Sorry.

How foolish of us to hope that babus can stop the loot of the exchequer or put their foot down when it comes to hare-brained policies such as demonetisation. Are our civil servants running the country or ruining the country?

To be fair to them, all civil servants are not civil serpents. Julio Ribeiro and K P S Gill ended terrorism in Punjab. When he had a free hand as Chief Election Commissioner, T N Seshan put the fear of god into politicians; Surat municipal commissioner S R Rao transformed the plague-scarred city from 'badsurat' to 'khubsurat'; Mumbai customs commissioner Daya Shankar was a terror to gold smugglers; Satish Sahney applied the healing touch to Mumbai as police chief after the post-Babri riots and serial blasts; N Vittal as

Central Vigilance Commissioner posted on the CVC website the names of 85 IAS and 22 IPS officers against whom the commission had sought criminal/departmental proceedings for major penalties; Rentala Chandrashekhar and J Satyanarayana pioneered e-governance in the country…

However, officers such as these are rare. Bureaucrats seem to have given up the fight against illegal orders by politicians. In the wake of the Hathras episode, 92 former civil servants collectively lamented "the meek surrender of the Uttar Pradesh bureaucracy and police, especially its All-India Services, to political diktat", adding that it had "shamed all of us who deem it a badge of honour to belong to these services".

What is needed though is a mechanism that wrests the absolute control of bureaucrats out of the hands of the political class. This is where initiatives such as the police reforms are so important. The Supreme Court passed direction in the Prakash Singh vs Union of India case way back in 2006 but police reforms remain largely unimplemented. The SC needs to call the Union home secretary and chief secretaries of the states to ensure compliance.

The IAS and IPS associations also can play a part by encouraging officers to do their work fearlessly but that has not happened. The reason is that most of the office-bearers, who are seniors, have made their compromises with the system. Youngsters join the civil services with idealism but over the years they lose much of their enthusiasm and innovativeness and end up as mere cogs in the wheel. A bureaucrat in the housing sector in Maharashtra once remarked in private that the policy was drafted by builders and all he had to do was to sign on the dotted line.

Many of these bureaucrats would have quit in disgust but they don't because they know that they won't be able to get a comparable job in the private sector. What competence or expertise can a civil servant hope to develop if he/she is transferred so often? And now there is a move for lateral entry by experts in various fields into civil services, a move seen with great suspicion by many.

Why shouldn't the government itself seek to create such specialists within the system? After some years of service, each officer can be encouraged to specialise in a sector by giving him/her a reasonably long tenure in it and permitting him/her to join an academic or research organisation for a year or two.

To its credit, the civil services have officers who have quit to do social work, such as Jayaprakash Narayan who formed the Lok Satta party to work on a grassroots movement for good governance, Aruna Roy who pioneered the RTI movement, and human rights activist Harsh Mander. The latest is Kannan Gopinathan, who resigned last year stating that he was disturbed over the denial of fundamental rights to lakhs of citizens in J&K. During the Kerala floods of 2018 he had worked incognito as a volunteer, even lifting sacks.

Just as the performers must be rewarded, the corrupt and the slackers must be compulsorily retired. The civil services cannot be a club for life. Also, the law insulating bureaucrats from prosecution without sanction deserves a serious relook.

PM Modi has sacked corrupt bureaucrats on more than one occasion but his mantra of 'minimum government and maximum governance' cannot work unless the rampant corruption in the lower bureaucracy is tackled. There is a cabal at all levels; village, tehsil, district and state; with politicians, the media and others in the criminal justice system protecting each other. The entire system turns against those who don't fall in line and whistle-blowers are implicated in fake or real cases.

More than the PM, it is up to the people and the media to expose wrongdoing and support upright bureaucrats and those working honestly but silently in the lower bureaucracy. Ultimately, as G B Shaw said, democracy is a device that ensures that we will be governed no better than we deserve.

* * *

Justice Prevails or Justices Prevail?

Over the years, the judiciary seems to have taken it as its right not to be criticised.

The Prashant Bhushan moment too shall pass for the Supreme Court but it will have to clear its name in the court of the people. The common man who looks up to the SC to protect his life and liberty has been watching events unfold at the apex court with a growing sense of disquiet.

A series of questionable actions and non-actions by the SC in recent years raise the suspicion in the minds of many that it is self-seeking, that instead of justice prevailing it is a case of justices prevailing and most damning, that it is pro-establishment.

It is a fairly long list but just take the way the sexual harassment case against Ranjan Gogoi was dealt with when he was the chief justice. It erased all the goodwill the SC had earned through its landmark Vishakha guidelines in 1997. If this was not a case of 'scandalizing the judiciary', what was it.

Take the way the SC was blind to the plight of urban workers trudging to their villages, take the way judges are driving students to examination centres when they themselves are ruling from the safety of their homes.

It is not only the common man who laments the decline in the quality of judges, former SC judge Madan Lokur is on record saying that the faith of the people in the judiciary has been shaken.

One of the measures of faith in the judiciary is the respect it commands; there has been minimal criticism of courts. The media is deferential and rarely blasts a bad judgment although it has every right to do so provided it does not attribute motives to it.

However, commanding respect and demanding respect are two different things. The media is also circumspect as it is fearful of judges invoking the dreaded Contempt of courts Act, 1971. Up to 2006, not even truth was a defence in contempt cases. No less a person than constitutional expert Fali Nariman is of the view that higher judiciary in India has unbridled power of contempt.

Over the years, the judiciary seems to have taken it as its right not to be criticised. Look at the Prashant Bhushan case where the SC frowned at even retired judges. Finding fault with the judiciary is almost like blasphemy; the media is deterred from reporting any judicial wrongdoing through the sweeping use of the contempt law. In most cases, a threat suffices. Why then denounce cops for 'danda raaj'?

Talking of cops, look at the gangster Vikas Dubey case. The police, the politicians and even the media came in for criticism but the judiciary escaped its share of the blame.

After all, Dubey's delusion that he was above the law took root in the courtroom where he was acquitted of killing a minister in a police station. The judge ought to have questioned how all the witnesses, including policemen, turned hostile. Now, was this not a fit case of 'lowering the majesty of the law'?

The higher judiciary took cognizance of it only after the Dubey encounter case reached the SC; terming the grant of parole by a court of law to the gangster despite 65 FIRs pending against him as 'institutional failure', the bench asked for all the orders passed by the trial courts in cases pertaining to Dubey.

Take the Jessica Lall case. Manu Sharma, son of a Haryana politico, was acquitted by the trial court of shooting dead the model in a packed high-society bar because she, one of the celebrity barmaids, denied him a drink after closing time. Yet, it was public outcry rather than a judicial review that put the rich brat behind bars. Do such things enhance the reputation of the judiciary which is otherwise so harsh on anyone 'bringing the judiciary into disrepute'?

Every other pillar of democratic governance except the judiciary is subject to some system of accountability and checks and balances. The judiciary though revels in remaining opaque and immune to scrutiny. Former SC judge Ruma Pal was forthright when she said that the normal response of courts to any enquiry about their functioning is to stonewall it.

Not only is the judiciary averse to criticism, it seems incapable of self-correction. Even SC judges had to hold a press conference in 2018 accusing Chief Justice Dipak Misra of manipulating the roster, thereby insinuating that cases were being assigned to preferred benches.

When was the last time that a SC judge was pulled up for misconduct? In fact, the in-house procedure supposed to enforce the code of ethics for judges is opaque and often dysfunctional.

In the absence of a law on judicial accountability, Pal suggests that formal internal mechanisms be set up for disciplining judges to ensure continued public confidence in the judicial system.

Perhaps we need a Performance Commission, as in several states in the US, which examine complaints about the conduct of judges and have powers to take consequential action.

There ought to be a system of analysing the quality of orders/judgments to determine the judges' competence and promotion. Quite a few are apparently just wasting time issuing interim orders.

Other worthwhile reform ideas are televising courtroom proceedings and the creation of a national judicial service from where the bulk of future judges could be selected.

The same judges who are quick to slap a contempt case on critics for scandalizing the judiciary see nothing wrong in some of their own accepting plum government posts the day they retire. Talk of intellectual integrity.

Today, those who have gamed the system proudly proclaim full faith in it. Litigants wonder why thundering statements by the judge in court are often not reflected in the written judgment or why some judges wake up to shake up the establishment only on their last day in office. Then there's the vexed issue of case law versus face law; children of sitting judges practicing in the same court.

Public acceptance is the bedrock of the judiciary's strength. Fortunately for it, despite everything people still trust the judiciary over the legislature and the executive. The Supreme Court of India is a powerful and magnificent machine – a Harley Davidson – and those astride it must ride responsibly.

Why Doesn't the Dam Water Reach the Taps?

Maharashtra accounts for one-third of the large dams in the country but its cities are forever thirsty.

With the onset of summer, there have been *'dharnas', 'morchas', 'gheraos'*, and PILs over water across Maharashtra. Protestors gathered at the Katraj pumping station were even caned by the Pune police. On the other hand, the Bombay High Court has ruled favourably on at least three PILs.

The state government has ruled out a water crisis this summer as its dams are more than half-full with just a month-and-a-half to go before the monsoon. If there's a slight worry, it is about Nagpur whose water reserves stand at 44 per cent. So, the crisis is really about distribution; India's classic last-mile connectivity problem.

Maharashtra, in fact, is the country's top dam builder. According to the National Register of Large Dams, Maharashtra has 1,845 dams, which account for 35 per cent of India's large dams. Madhya Pradesh comes a distant second with 906 dams.

A large dam, going by the National Register of Large Dams, is defined as one with a height of more than 15 metres or a storage capacity of more than 60 million cubic metres. Dams with heights between 10-15 metres are also included in the list.

Despite having the largest number of big dams in the country, most cities in Maharashtra are dependent on water tankers.

Credit: Prashant Nakwe

If Maharashtra's cities, excluding Mumbai, are clamouring for water, it is because not enough money and mind have been spent on the issue. There are just not enough pipelines from the dams to the cities and within the cities themselves. The apathy of the ruling elite, which is concerned only about irrigating its sugarcane crop, was evident in Deputy CM Ajit Pawar's crass humour in 2013. "If there's no water in the dam, how can we release it? Should we urinate in it?", he had said at a rally in rural Pune, referring to the hunger strike by a Solapur farmer demanding more water. Pawar later apologised for the remark.

He fancies himself as the strong man of Pune but is mum on its water woes. Punekars complain that several areas have to depend on expensive tanker water despite paying water taxes while all the five lakes around the city have sufficient water.

Virtually every housing society in Baner, Pashan, Balewadi is dependent on water tankers, some throughout the year. Housing societies in the affected areas spend 90 per cent of their maintenance charges on buying tanker water.

Pune residents have questioned the mandate of 'water affidavits' sought from builders by the Pune Municipal Corporation (PMC).

Such is the situation that the PMC is planning to challenge the Bombay HC order telling them to supply tanker water to the residents in the 23 merged villages. PMC says that providing water to the eight lakh residents will need 4,500 tankers and incur a cost of Rs 200 cr per annum.

Meanwhile, the state irrigation department has warned the PMC that it is overdrawing water to the detriment of agriculture. By the way, despite the dams, only 18 per cent of the land that is tilled in Maharashtra is irrigated. The national average is 45 per cent.

Nagpur residents have been complaining that only 20 per cent of the city gets a satisfactory water supply despite spending Rs 1,100 cr over the past ten years. After a public outcry, the Nagpur civic chief has ordered a third-party audit of Orange City Water, a private firm tasked with uninterrupted water supply.

In Aurangabad, a rising industrial hub, residents get water once in five days. There was a flurry of activity only after the HC, hearing a PIL, asked for a weekly update on the situation. Now, it appears that there are only three km of pipes for the proposed pipeline from the Jayakwadi dam, 40 km away. How ironic that just last fortnight, all these three cities were collecting some prize or the other at the Smart Cities award function at Surat.

There is a general disinterest in the state machinery when it comes to the water supply. Aurangabad's otherwise dynamic civic chief Astik Kumar Pandey got going only when Industries minister Subhash Desai, the guardian minister of Aurangabad, was miffed with the slow pace of work on the Rs 1,670 cr water pipeline project for the city.

It seems that the city's hydraulic engineers just do not have the expertise or the experience to execute the project which involves creating an efficient network to distribute an additional 100 MLD of water from Jayakwadi dam. Now, IIT-Powai has been appointed as the project management consultant. For good measure, the minister has suggested that BMC's hydraulic engineers can provide some tips.

In civic circles, it is said that those transferred from the lucrative departments to the water department lose all interest in work. After a surprise visit to the N-5 apartments in the CIDCO area, Pandey issued show-cause notices to three assistant engineers who were not taking the water crisis there seriously despite a '*dharna*' by the residents.

Incidentally, water supply to the world heritage Ajanta Caves has been discontinued since 2019 for non-payment of dues.

Nowhere is the inefficiency of civic bodies so cruelly exposed as in water supply in the summer months. In Baramati, which has a problem of plenty, the civic authorities were unaware that the SCADA system – a mix of software and hardware elements that monitors, gathers, and processes real-time data — of the water purification unit had been stolen.

Sudhir Bhongale, an expert on water resources, says that urban planners must pay urgent attention to upgrading the water network. He also wants the authorities to stop the uncontrolled sand mining which is robbing the rivers of water holding capacity and leading to the drying up of wells.

Our attitudes too are to blame. Those who get regular piped water do not value it. For instance, the residents of Navi Mumbai revolted when the civic chief suggested that the city could save water by stopping the supply for one day in the evening. Perhaps it is time to look at charging higher rates for those who can afford it and penalising its wastage, something that Bhongale also recommends.

As Union Jal Shakti minister Gajendra Shekhawat said recently, in Mumbai, there is a dire need for water literacy.

Is the Doctor Feeling Your Pulse or Your Purse?

The patient cannot be treated like a commodity.

Whom do doctors go to when they fall ill? And do they take the same medicines and tests that they prescribe to us? Answering these questions may help heal the delicate doctor-patient relationship which suffered another setback last week.

It started with Mumbai's new police commissioner Sanjay Pandey warning doctors not to prescribe unnecessary tests for the sake of a commission from the diagnostic labs. "The person coming to you has a serious problem, you cannot treat him like a commodity," he said in his weekly social media address. The Association of Medical Consultants demanded that he withdraw the remarks. Other doctors called his statement a downright attack on the medical profession.

As usual, the truth is somewhere in the middle. And the onus of dealing with it is on the medical profession. Pandey, a public-spirited bureaucrat, was just articulating people's feelings in his normal blunt manner. While there are dedicated doctors, there are also those who exploit a patient's faith in the noble profession. Complicating the equation are some unscrupulous private hospitals that milk the patient as well as the doctor but more about that later.

The basic problem is with the doctor-patient relationship. Patients feel that doctors have no time to listen to them, that empathy is missing, and that they are happy prescribing a plethora of medicines and running a gamut of tests on them instead of hearing them out and examining them in some detail. In short, the doctor has no patience. Also, doctors never admit that some ailments can be treated better by alternate therapy.

Sadly, this happens in all professions, there are just too many anecdotal cases to dismiss it as deviant behaviour. I can reel out a few personal cases but let me narrate just one concerning my late father. After retirement, he trekked to Chhota Kailash during which he once experienced sharp pain in the chest. Attributing it to exhaustion, he moved on after resting a day or two. On returning home to Mumbai a month or so later, he saw the family doctor who ran an ECG which showed that he had suffered a minor heart attack. The doctor advised him to get admitted immediately to the ICU at a particular hospital. My father ignored it, reasoning that if he could survive two months in the hills and a long train journey home, he wasn't going to die in a day. He took his own time and a second opinion and lived for two decades without any sign of heart trouble. Now, every case is different from the other but knowing both parties, I am inclined to believe that in this case, it was a 'different' doctor.

Arguing for doctors, who are often bad communicators, one can say that patients expect a pill for every illness and feel that an injection is a better option. Over the years, patients have been conditioned to believe that doctors who do not give lengthy prescriptions are not qualified enough.

Patients can be such hypochondriacs that they google out the symptoms and want the doctor to confirm their diagnosis! Given their busy schedule, doctors don't suffer such fools gladly. It is also irrational on the patient's part to attribute every death to negligence on the part of doctors. This could be one reason why doctors prescribe a battery of tests as defensive medicine. However, there is no denying the existence of the pernicious 'cut' practice.

Most experts agree that healthcare fraud is rampant in India, with recent corruption scandals engulfing everyone from doctors to drug companies and health regulators. In 2013, Dr H S Bawaskar, who runs a hospital in Raigad, filed a complaint with the Maharashtra Medical

Council with documentary proof of a diagnostic centre sending him a "cut" for referring his patients to it for scanning.

Dr Arun Gadre, a gynaecologist-turned-health activist, says three types of malpractice are particularly common: kickbacks for referrals, irrational drug prescribing, and unnecessary interventions. One of the 78 doctors he interviewed told him that doctors typically get Rs 30,000 to 40,000 for referring patients for angioplasty. And this was ten years ago.

This was what Sanjay Pandey was referring to when he said that in COVID times diagnostic companies had made mind-boggling amounts of money with tests that doctors prescribed. Here, one must also mention that as many as 67 doctors died due to COVID-19 in Maharashtra.

The medical profession is getting a bad name mainly because of corporate hospitals, where doctors are given targets and patients are overbilled. If doctors fail to meet the targets, they are punished, and if they exceed the targets they are rewarded. Some years ago, the Kokilaben Dhirubhai Ambani Hospital in Mumbai was hauled up for proposing an "Elite Forum for Doctors" where doctors would be rewarded with money for referring patients to the hospital.

During COVID, these hospitals forgot all humanity and fleeced patients. Based on the complaints of patients, the Maharashtra government scrutinised thousands of bills and refunded more than Rs 35 crores to them.

The onus to improve the doctor-patient relationship is ultimately on the individuals. Dr Behram Pardiwala, a consultant at leading Mumbai hospitals, has a word of advice for young doctors: "One must always look at a patient as the doctor would if it was his family member. It is important to understand the patient's suffering and then move forward with the treatment. But young doctors lack this; they just see a patient as a job for which they are getting paid a certain sum of money."

He was merely repeating the 17th-century Italian physician Giorgio Baglivi: "Let the young know they will never find a more interesting, more instructive book than the patient himself."

✳ ✳ ✳

Mumbai Police: Scotland Yard to Market Yard

It is not every day that the home minister is publicly accused of extortion by the police commissioner.

The political whodunit in Maharashtra is unfolding so rapidly that everyone missed a moment of supreme irony; initiating damage control early on, NCP leader Sharad Pawar suggested an inquiry headed by Julio Ribeiro, one of Mumbai's best remembered police chiefs.

Now, Ribeiro has been a votary of police professionalism for three decades but no one paid any heed. On the contrary, Mumbai has seen a succession of tainted police commissioners. Finally, when things went awry and one such commissioner spilled the beans, politicians began looking for someone with credibility, not for the commissioner's post but for a whitewash job!

As expected, Ribeiro scoffed at the offer, saying that he would not touch it with a barge pole. Squarely blaming the politicians, he said that the mess was of their own making and that they ought to sort it out themselves.

One can say that the ruling coalition, the Maha Vikas Aghadi (MVA), was taken by surprise; it is not every day that the home minister is publicly accused of extortion by a top cop. Here, the cop, Parambir Singh, also challenged his removal as Mumbai police commissioner.

Danda raj at the bottom and goonda raj at the top sullied the image of the Mumbai police.
Credit: Sudharak Olwe

There were rumblings of discontent in the top echelons of the Maharashtra police but the novice CM failed to notice them. In December, Subodh Kumar Jaiswal, who enjoys a clean image, quit midway through his term as the Director-General to take up a central government assignment. This was unprecedented but bigger shocks were in store.

Jaiswal was not as noisy as Singh was to be but as a parting shot he let it be known that his report on the practice of lobbying for posts was dumped by the government. Instead of taking corrective action, home minister Anil Deshmukh went for the whitewash option; a meeting with former state police chiefs to improve the image of the Maharashtra police.

All this while, Sanjay Pandey, another public-spirited officer with a squeaky clean reputation, had been reminding the government that as the state's seniormost IPS officer he deserved a better posting than the one at the home guards. When he was given another insignificant posting as chief of the State Security Commission, Pandey lashed out at the government in an open letter, revealing, among other things, embarrassing details of official inquiries he had been assigned to.

However, the IPS volcano truly erupted two days later on March 20 with Parambir releasing a letter that singed the MVA government. Parambir may well have been a scapegoat in the Antilia case but the last straw for him was public humiliation; Deshmukh blamed him on TV saying he had committed 'unpardonable' mistakes.

This was a deplorable lack of finesse on the minister's part. Politicians feel that they can ride roughshod over the bureaucracy without inviting a backlash. Sharad Pawar himself as CM had announced the transfer of Sanjay Pandey, then deputy commissioner of the Dharavi zone, at a press conference. However, he had the good sense to cancel it when several citizens' groups came out in support of Pandey.

Normally, an astute administrator like Pawar would have sensed the danger afoot. After all, this is the same man who fifteen years ago had spoken disparagingly about the 'transfer industry'.

Now, damaging details of the Jaiswal report are being read out in the assembly by the leader of the opposition, Devendra Fadnavis.

Officers 'purchase' lucrative postings but the price is ultimately paid by the citizens. Needless to say, only the dishonest have the money to bid for postings. Has anyone asked why 26/11 hero Sadanand Date heads the insignificant coastal commissionerate and not Pune, Thane or Navi Mumbai?

IPS officers who buy plum postings rake it in with impunity; their 'collection agents' are an open secret. One such officer who was posted to Navi Mumbai set monthly 'collection' targets for all the police stations despite the fat earnings from the town's dance bars. And all this happened under the late R R Patil as home minister.

Dance bars were such a corrupting influence on the cops that an upright deputy commissioner in Mumbai had to bypass the police station hierarchy and send fresh recruits to monitor their timings. During one of his night rounds, this DCP, now a top cop, was perhaps mistaken for the local inspector by a dance bar owner who not only abused him but also raised his hand on him; Mumbai's Vikas Dubey moment.

Nightlife is a big source of earnings for cops and their masters which is why it faces no curbs even when COVID is spiking.

Not only do rogue cops book businessmen under false charges, there have been instances of cops turning highway robbers and kidnappers. Those thus kidnapped have been hidden in the office of at least one Mumbai DCP. These criminals in uniform make a mockery of the Maharashtra police motto: *Sadrakshanaya khalnighrahanaya* (protector of the law-abiding and annihilator of the evil).

The Telgi fake stamp paper scam where several senior police officers were arrested is fresh in memory. The joke at the time was that it is possible to form a commissionerate in jail.

On the other hand, the handful of honest officers who have got executive postings without lobbying are afraid that their corrupt colleagues will conspire to get them out on false charges. One only has to read former IPS officer Y P Singh's book, '*Carnage by angels*' to know how the system works.

The posting-transfer industry can be traced back to the time when coalition governments were formed in Maharashtra. According to Y P Singh, today all fear of the law has vanished and an extortion industry too is flourishing.

Postings right down to the constable are on sale. The going rate for the inspector in charge of a busy railway police station in Mumbai is Rs 50 lakh. Corrupt cops also need not fear adverse remarks in their annual confidential reports, the minister expunges them.

The systemic corruption in the Mumbai traffic police was exposed when head constable Sunil Toke filed a PIL in 2017 alleging rampant corruption and even providing a rate card. But why talk about traffic cops when politicians make money even in the purchase of bullet-proof vests and CCTVs.

There was a time when the 'encounter specialists', having amassed cash and clout through encounters (mostly contract killings on behalf of rival gangsters), became a force within a force.

There are honest officers at every police station but they are wary of becoming a 'Velankar', the frustrated sub-inspector who takes to alcohol; Om Puri in the Govind Nihalani classic, '*Ardha Satya*'.

Mumbai and Maharashtra have seen several public-spirited commissioners and DGs since Ribeiro's time; to name a few: D S Soman, Vasant Saraf, Satish Sahney, Arvind Inamdar, A N Roy, Ronald Mendonca, K Subramanyam, Sanjeev Dayal, Ahmad Javed and Dattatray Padsalgikar. The acting DGP Rajnish Seth too is a conscientious cop.

The list would be longer and the force more citizen-friendly had police reforms insulating cops from political interference been implemented. Today, the Mumbai police, which was once compared to the Scotland Yard is a market yard.

Section 9

Future Shock

What the Graying of India Means for Us

By 2050, one in every five Indians will be above 60.

If the young are struggling to keep their heads above the water during the pandemic, spare a thought for senior citizens living on their own. Out of sync, out of breath, out of money, they are best out of sight. Comeuppance for the I-me-myself generation is not far though. One in ten Indians is above the age of 60 but by 2050, when this generation approaches retirement, one in every five Indians will be above 60.

It has somehow escaped us that the decadal growth rate of the elderly population is nearly five times that of the general population. In the near future, this graying of the population will mean having to adjust to a new reality. There will be more dependents on fewer earning members, more elderly and fewer younger care-givers. Besides, because of the falling birth rate, many schools will have to be merged as there won't be enough children in one school. The change is already visible in the way more and more products for senior citizens are being marketed, from reverse mortgage to hearing aids to adult diapers.

The more we care for our elders and the better we prepare for an ageing population, the easier it will be for us to negotiate our own future. It is to highlight such issues that August 21 is observed as the World Senior Citizen's Day.

With rising life spans – the life expectancy in India is 69 years — and falling birth rates, the percentage of the elderly in the global population is rising; there are currently around 700 million people over the age of 60 and the figure is expected to touch two billion by 2050. This will be over 20 per cent of the world's population.

This alarming forecast prompted various initiatives to address the problems that will arise. The earliest was the Vienna Plan of Action on Ageing, 1982, which aimed at strengthening the capacities of governments and civil society to deal effectively with the graying of nations. To meet the dependency needs of older persons, it focused on health and nutrition, protection of elderly consumers, housing and environment, family, social welfare, income security and employment and education.

Change, however, is slow and wags say that there is no respect for age unless it is bottled. In India, the aged are at the mercy of their children. The government too has washed its hands of the issue by putting the onus on the children alone through the Maintenance and Welfare of Parents and Senior Citizens Act, 2007, which makes it obligatory for children and heirs to provide maintenance to their parents.

A survey by the non-government organisation, HelpAge India, in 2014 showed that only 0.5 per cent of elderly in Mumbai availed of benefits under this Act. This points to elder abuse, an open secret in Indian society. According to a recent survey conducted by HelpAge India, 62 per cent of senior citizens said that COVID had increased the risk of elder abuse. According to Census-2011, almost 15 million elderly Indians live all alone and close to three-fourths of them are women.

Incidentally, senior citizens accounted for around 63 per cent of all Covid-related deaths in the country. The graying of the population is more pronounced in the southern states, more notably Kerala and Tamil Nadu. Senior citizens constituted 12.6 per cent of Kerala's population in 2011 and today the figure is estimated to have climbed up to 16.5 per cent. Projections are that 20.9 per cent of the state's population will be aged 60 years or above in 2031. It is also projected that more than 15 per cent of the population of Andhra Pradesh, Karnataka, Odisha, Punjab and West Bengal will be aged 60 years and above in 2031.

As against this, only 7.7 per cent of Bihar's population and 8.1 per cent of Uttar Pradesh's are likely to be 60 years and above in 2031. Other states with less than 10 per cent of their population aged 60 years and above include Assam, Chhattisgarh, Jharkhand, Madhya Pradesh and Rajasthan.

Most of the elderly are poor and many spend a disproportionate amount of their savings on medical expenses. There was a case in Warangal where an 83-year-old man killed his 78-year-old ailing wife and attempted commit suicide. He had tended to her for three months. The police said that he was struggling to pay for her medical expenses, which is what drove him to desperation.

The National Programme for Healthcare of Elderly, launched in 2010, could have come to his rescue but it remains largely on paper. Even pensioners have been hit hard by the rock-bottom bank interest rates and soaring inflation, not to speak of inflated electricity bills. Even for the well-off, medicare for the aged is primitive. Gerontology, the study of the aged population, is still in its nascent stages in the country, which means that there aren't enough doctors who specialise in elder care.

A study by the International Institute for Population Sciences, Mumbai, in collaboration with several national and international institutions revealed that 75 per cent of the elderly in India suffer from one or the other chronic disease, 40 per cent have one or the other disability and 20 per cent have issues related to mental health.

Of course, if you are healthy, age is just a number and you are only as old as you feel. In fact, scientists say our biological potential is 130 years, which means that we reach our middle age only at 70 and that the forties are the best time of our youth. One only has to look at our *'rishis'* to validate this.

Indian society needs to be sensitised to ageing so that they keep themselves physically and fiscally fit for their second innings. Policy-makers too have been urged to prepare for an ageing population by the Economic Survey 2018-19, which says this will need investment in health care as well as a plan for increasing the retirement age in a phased manner. The middle-aged have to seriously consider re-skilling themselves for a second career to sustain themselves after retirement.

It can be a cruel world for the elderly and we need to address the issue of ageing today; individually and collectively. Tomorrow will be too late.

Plunder Till You Blunder, Now Taste the Thunder

Flash floods are Nature's mild warning for our avarice and arrogance.

Ancient texts the world over ascribe floods to the wrath of the gods. It rings true even in this era of spaceflights and cloud computing. How otherwise does one explain the havoc wrought by just two days of unseasonal rain in states as disparate as Kerala and Uttarakhand? Flash floods are in fact a global phenomenon; Nature's mild warning for our avarice and arrogance.

So, let's try and understand where we have gone wrong. Simply said, our planet is warming up too fast; the current global average temperature is 0.85° C higher than it was in the late 19th century, mainly because of carbon dioxide released from the burning of oil, gas, and coal. Now, CO_2 acts like the glass in a greenhouse; trapping the sun's heat and stopping it from leaking back into space. As the earth's atmosphere heats up, it collects, retains and drops more water, changing weather patterns.

The increasing number of erratic rainfall events in India is in line with the predictions made by the UN's Intergovernmental Panel on Climate Change (IPCC), which has been providing global-scale assessments of the earth's climate every five to seven years since 1988, focusing on changes in temperature and ice cover, greenhouse gas emissions, and sea levels across the planet.

Last year, the IPCC predicted that India would see even further acceleration in the recession of the glaciers and snow caps in the Himalayas across the 21ˢᵗ century. As temperatures increase, glaciers will melt and shrink and the area covered with snow will decrease significantly. At the same time, rainfall is expected to intensify across the Himalayan region. Noted Indian glaciologist D P Dobhal says that over the last 50 years, the snowline has gone up from 4,800 metres to 5,200 metres. Also, the average temperature in the Himalayas has risen by 0.3 to 0.6° C over the last century.

Likewise, Roxy Koll, a climate scientist with the Indian Institute of Tropical Meteorology, Pune, says that the temperature over the Arabian Sea has increased by 1.2 to 1.4° C in the last two decades.

According to a study last year by Climate Central, a US non-profit news organisation comprising scientists and journalists, the sea level is rising and Mumbai, Kolkata, Chennai and Surat face the threat of submergence by 2050.

However, accepting the reality of climate change, global warming, melting polar caps, shrinking glaciers, rising sea levels is expecting too much from our politicians who have not yet acknowledged the exodus of migrant labour, the oxygen shortage or Lakhimpur Kheri. Their attitude is typified by PM Narendra Modi, who once dismissed climate change as something imaginary.

The Central government says that it has found no direct link between climate change and cloudbursts. Minister of State for Environment, Forests and Climate Change Ashwini Kumar Choubey told the Rajya Sabha in a written reply on August 2 this year that "there is no established study in India for estimating the quantified contribution of climate change in triggering cloudbursts".

Perhaps this is why our weather forecasting systems are not precise. And thanks to the 'whether' bureaus we are never ready for the first heavy showers. Mumbai's Doppler radar – which detects cloud formation, rain and thunderstorms – was out of order throughout this monsoon. This, in a city where over 400 perished on July 26, 2005, in a deluge caused by the heaviest rainfall witnessed in a century. This also explains our lackadaisical attitude to environmental issues. See how we have diluted the Coastal Regulation

Zone laws and are now tampering with the buffer zone around forests. We learn no lessons. And nothing's sacrosanct.

Whatever the minister says, the IMD and the Indian Institute of Tropical Meteorology attribute the increasing incidents of heavy rainfall in short spells to the climate crisis. In the last three years, Kerala has seen at least four flash floods, of which the 2018 floods were the worst, claiming around 400 lives. According to the IMD, Uttarakhand has reported over 7,750 extreme rainfall events and cloudbursts since 2015 – most of them in the last three years.

When dense rain clouds run into a mountain range, as in Uttarakhand and Kerala, it results in higher precipitation and quicker funnelling of water downstream, creating flash floods. To make it worse, we are indiscriminately quarrying hills, destabilising slopes by cutting hills for roads, building hydel power projects in fragile Himalayan valleys and stripping rivers of sand. The Char Dham National Highway linking Rishikesh to Mana is in full swing despite being flagged off by environmentalists as a Himalayan blunder.

In Maharashtra, floods this July caused so much damage mainly because the previous government did away with the river regulation policy forbidding construction along the banks. The Western Ghats, running from Maharashtra to Kerala, are one of the world's ten biodiversity hotspots – just this month five species of freshwater crabs were discovered there – but we want to set up thermal and nuclear power plants, refineries, chemical zones, open cast mines and what not in this ecologically fragile strip.

In his prophetic book, *'Flood and Fury'*, journalist Viju B has detailed the ecological devastation of the Western Ghats. The once-in-a-century explanation of the Kerala government for the 2018 floods, he says, was washed away the very next year when 76 people were killed in Wayanad and Malappuram.

The Uttarakhand and Kerala flash floods toll touched 100 but since most of us don't experience the impact directly it is difficult to fully comprehend the consequences of the climate crisis. Hence, the Mila-Quebec Artificial Intelligence Institute has developed a tool that makes it possible to visualise the effects of floods, wildfires and smog anywhere in the world. For instance, based on the rate of the sea-level rise off the coast of Mumbai – 1.7

mm per year – it can show you how Nariman Point will look after 30 years. If only our politicians had heard about it.

But what each one of us can do is to focus on the green mantra, 'Think global, act local'. We can make our neighbourhood more liveable. Take inspiration from Gaura Devi and the other village women of the '*Chipko andolan*', who hugged trees in Uttarakhand to save them from the timber mafia.

Emulate teenager Aditya Mukarji, who convinced over 150 restaurants, hotels and institutions in Gurugram to go plastic-free in 2018. Learn from the morning walkers at Mumbai's Sanjay Gandhi national park who banded together in 2011 to clean the four rivers that flow out of the park. Over the years, their River March movement has become a pilgrimage for nature enthusiasts.

Only when citizens act will climate change get any traction. Otherwise, the media will be obsessed with Aryan Khan, with the furore over the use of Urdu in a Diwali advertisement by Fabindia and with human rights being 'misused' to defame India. Mumbai-2005 is history and Kedarnath-2013, Chennai-2015 and even Chiplun-2021 are distant memories; not acts of God but the avarice of man.

Section 10

The Way We Are

A Check-up from the Neck Up

*The Sushant Singh Rajput suicide case underlines the need for
mental health awareness.*

The last hit Sushant Singh Rajput starred in, *Chhichhore*, had a message about suicide prevention, so when the actor took his own life, his fans were unable to reconcile with it. The speculation over the rising star's death only shows how little the general public knows about mental health.

After his death, it came to light that Sushant was under treatment for bipolar disorder, a mental health condition characterized by extreme mood swings, emotional highs and lows. During the low phase, the patient may have overwhelming feelings of worthlessness, which can potentially lead to thoughts of suicide.

Yet, Sushant's fans went by his public persona of an optimist bubbling with energy and started seeing conspiracy theories. Fanned by the media and fed by our prejudices, these theories have now taken hold of the public imagination as 'truth stranger than fiction'. Or, one can say, a narcotic-altered reality.

Instead of chasing the conspiracy theories, news TV channels could do well to look at mental health, at least on September 10, which is World Suicide Prevention Day.

It is time we woke up to the reality that India is not only in the middle of a recession but also in the middle of a mental health epidemic. According to the Indian Council of Medical Research, one in seven Indians suffers from some kind of mental ailment which includes depression, anxiety disorders, schizophrenia, bipolar disorders, dissociative identity disorders and autism. Add the stress caused by COVID-'19 to this 2017 study and the picture worsens.

The first step to fighting mental illness is to de-stigmatize it; Indians are generally not supportive of a co-worker struggling with a mental ailment because they associate it with madness. Their employers should come forward and say that mental illness is curable just like any physical illness. It is another matter that workplace stress accounted for one-fourth of the suicides in India last year.

Ironically, old Hindi films are responsible for the worst stereotypes when it comes to mental illness; they make a laughing stock out of such patients. Now, compare this with the Hollywood films, '*One flew over the cuckoo's nest*' in 1975 on a psychiatric ward or the 2001 film, '*A beautiful mind*', which depicts the true-life story of mathematician John Nash who battled schizophrenia — a disorder that affects a person's ability to think, feel and behave clearly — and even went on to win the Nobel prize.

Perhaps inspired by these classics, Bollywood has come up with a slew of realistic films on mental ailments; '*Black*', which was about Alzheimer's disease, '*Kartik calling Kartik*', '*Woh Lamhe*' and '*15 Park Avenue*', all three on schizophrenia, '*Taare Zameen Par*' on autism, '*Dear Zindagi*' which showed how stress and unhappiness can result in insomnia, and '*Bhool Bhulaiyaa*', which was about dissociative identity disorder or multiple personality disorder.

The second step to fighting mental disorder is to recognize the symptoms such as long-lasting sadness or irritability, extreme mood swings, excessive fear, worry, or anxiety, social withdrawal or drastic changes in eating or sleeping habits.

In joint families, elders picked up the signals and counselled younger members but with nuclear families the only option is mental health literacy which encompasses recognition, causes, self-help and facilitation of professional intervention.

In fact, family problems are the major reason for suicide in India – one third of all cases — according to the National Crime Records Bureau. The same report by the NCRB notes that a quarter of the suicides last year, or 32,563 of the total 1,39,123, are by daily-wage earners.

City dwellers can seek help from mental health helplines but debt-ridden small farmers are left to deal on their own with corrosive despair. It is heartening that the National Institute for Mental Health and Neuro-Sciences (NIMHANS) has launched a national helpline (080-46110007) to provide counselling on mental health and psycho-social issues related to the pandemic and lockdown.

Tragic as every suicide is, the ones by celebrities serve to focus attention on mental health. Take the case of filmmaker Guru Dutt, known for classics such as 'Kaagaz ke phool', 'Pyaasa' and 'Sahib, bibi aur gulam' who was depressed and succeeded in taking his life with an overdose of sleeping pills in 1964.

His cinematographer and close associate V K Murthy said in an interview that this was his third attempt. The last straw for him, Murthy indicated, was that his close friends were going away upon retirement or on work.

However, one of Guru Dutt's relatives who was to join Bollywood managed to beat depression — Deepika Padukone. She runs a foundation for mental health and has been sharing must-read notes on social media in her attempt to normalise conversation around mental health.

The World Suicide Prevention Day gives organizations, government agencies and individuals a chance to promote awareness about suicide, mental illnesses associated with suicide, as well as suicide prevention.

Fans of Sushant Singh Rajput can pay homage to his memory by sparing a moment to go through the pieces on mental health published on this day. It can save another Sushant.

* * *

Affluenza & the New Year Murder

---

*Children need and want to be told right from wrong and learn responsibility
and the consequences of their actions.*

A bunch of Mumbai teenagers have a terrace party to ring in the New Year but it ends with one of them dead and two of them arrested for murder. Now, suspicion of drugs, sex and a love triangle make the case more gripping than any Netflix thriller.

However, salacious speculation must not overshadow the fact that these are students and there was no plot. It's easy to blame youngsters but the others – parents, teachers, neighbours and the community — cannot escape responsibility. There is no point saying what's wrong with today's kids, this is as much a case of what's wrong with society.

The victim, a 19-year-old psychology student, was to enrol in an Australian college while the two suspects were her close friends; a 22-year-old boy who studies at a reputed catering college and the girl next-door to her, with whom she had started a baking venture during the lockdown.

These are upper-middle-class kids from suburban Mumbai and if it wasn't for a moment of mad rage they would have gone on unnoticed to become regular grown-ups fretting about raising teenagers.

Who hasn't been a bit wild in their youth? Bill Gates, one of the richest, was booked for speeding and driving without a licence when he was 19, British actor Stephen Fry was arrested at 17 for credit card fraud; he had been misusing a family friend's card for three months. Former U S President

Bill Clinton admitted to smoking pot as a student though he clarified clumsily that he did not inhale it.

Closer home, there's Sanjay Dutt who has made a movie out of his days as a junkie and his time behind bars for keeping an AK-47 rifle. Early in his career, cricketer-turned-politician Navjote Singh Sidhu was involved in a road rage incident that resulted in a death. There are umpteen such cases – from drugs to shootings to rape and murder — which are hushed up in India. An exception was the Jessica Lal case, for which rich brat Manu Sharma spent time in jail.

Coming back to the terrace party, it is said to have started at 7.30 pm and gone on till 1.30 am – six hours. How many parents, especially fathers, spend even 15 minutes a day of quality time with their college-going kids? Imagine the disconnect where family dinners have been replaced by solo TV dinners. As it is, the social secrets of teens go deeper than parents think.

Where's the family bonding, the reverence for life, the respect for the law and the obligation to society? Are we as parents, elders and teachers able to instill these values in children? Instead, public school brats treat their teachers like their employees.

Who are their role-models? A Salman Khan who is 'Being Human' after crushing human beings, a foul-mouthed Virat Kohli who calls it aggression or someone like Sundar Pichai of Google or Gita Gopinath, chief economist of the International Monetary Fund? Parents are the first role models for children but how many live up to expectations. Most can't even be friends with them.

Why is it that most of us cannot think of partying without intoxicants, that too which we cannot handle responsibly? Why can't conversation flow instead of alcohol? In fact, people these days cannot make a point without getting provoked and personal. If grown-ups do not know how to socialise, how can they expect it from their kids?

Children need and want to be told right from wrong and learn responsibility and the consequences of their actions. However, parents tend to be either very strict or very lax. No parent dropped in to check on the party, including that of the boy who had organized the party attended by 13 people and who lives in the same building.

Diagnosing the malaise, psychiatrist Alex Martin says our children who are supposed to be hand-held while they explore their world are left to face the adult world guided not by parents and teachers, but by the social media, resulting in ill-founded relationships, a crass understanding of sexuality, reality mired by drugs and a digital world which is cold and emotionally hollow.

Tell-tale tufts of hair and blood stains were found in the staircase on the second floor but strangely no one heard any screams from the scuffle between the deceased and the arrested duo, not even the watchman. The victim's body was discovered on the ground floor by the dog of a resident who was seeing off a guest around 2.30 am.

After the scuffle, the victim's friends — the duo who have been arrested — abandoned her, letting her bleed to death from a fractured skull, while they got themselves treated for their injuries.

The victim's family first learnt about something having gone wrong only at 5 am when their next-door neighbour called saying there had been an accident involving their daughters. Strangely, none of them thought of their daughters till then. And they are from a generation where girls were expected to be home by 7 pm (*'Saat chya aat gharat'*).

Yet, this is a relatively simple case. Adolescents and teenagers from respectable families have been involved in far more heinous crimes. In 2003, five innocent-looking local boys from the Goan community murdered Leticia Mendes and her toddler grandson in IC colony, Borivli, Mumbai.

In 2012, Sandhya Singh, sister of yesteryear Bollywood actresses Sulakshana Pandit and Vijeta Pandit, was strangled by her drug addict son who dissolved her body in acid in the bathtub and dumped her skeleton in the marshes 200 metres away from their house in NRI Complex, Navi Mumbai.

In 2015 in Mumbai, a 15-year-old Malad girl was gang-raped by a classmate and three of his friends who made video clips of the crime. Seven-year-old Pradhyumn Thakur of Gurugram's Ryan International School was murdered in the school toilet in 2017 by a class XI student in the hope that the exams would be postponed.

The culture of entitlement makes today's kids feel they can do anything and get away with it, says psychiatrist Dayal Mirchandani. The I-me-myself generation also does not think about the consequences.

In the US, there's a term for delinquent behaviour by the wealthy – affluenza. It is defined as the inability of individuals to understand the consequences of their actions because of their social status and/or financial privilege.

The term gained currency when a Texas teenager who mowed down four pedestrians while driving drunk in 2013 was sentenced to ten years of probation and zero jail time after his attorney successfully argued that his privileged upbringing precluded his ability to understand the consequences of his actions.

It's time for us also to wake up to affluenza and do something about the problems of the poor little rich kids before they become everyone's problems.

Architecture or Soulless Structures?

---

*Bad architecture and design are robbing Indian cities of all
character and charm.*

Most people must have wondered what the fuss over demolishing some dormitories in IIM, Ahmedabad, is all about, why the move to replace them with new buildings is being opposed at all. The answer is, architecture.

The problem is that most Indians don't know what architecture really is, having lived and worked in drab cuboid buildings all their lives.

Architecture is more than just the built environment, it is a representation of how we see ourselves as well as how we see the world.

We even seem to have forgotten our legacy; from the Sun temple at Konark to the Meenakshi temple of Madurai, to step wells such as the *Rani ni Vaav* in Patan, Gujarat, to magnificent Rajasthani places and forts to the Taj Mahal.

Architecture has been described as frozen music, an expression of values, the quest for the truth and inhabited sculpture. But how are we to appreciate it if even apartments costing Rs 5 cr don't have the basics such as cross-ventilation. Cross-ventilation, in fact, has gone out of the window.

Coming back to IIM, Ahmedabad, which is universally recognized as one of the best institutional buildings. Designed by acclaimed American architect Louis Kahn, its cylindrical towers, vaulted corridors and geometric play of light and shadow make it a masterpiece.

The red-brick campus with its spartan residential dorms with a play of light and shade, mass and void, the built and the open have been likened to the monastic cells of Ajanta and Ellora. The interplay between architectural design and human psychology, totally ignored today, had been used by the early Buddhists who made these rock-cut monasteries.

Architect Narayan Moorthy of LokPATH India, a citizens' collective of architects, urban planners, environmentalists and social activists that seeks appropriate transformations of habitat, says the IIM-A campus displays the uncanny intuitive ability of a foreign mind to respond to India's unique light, climate and social mores and thus remains a place of pilgrimage for architects and aesthetes.

One only has to compare it with other college campuses to realize what is wrong with Indian architecture today. In fact, the evidence is all around.

Just look at the hideous buildings in the business hubs of Mumbai at Nariman Point, BKC and Lower Parel. Is there one building which stands out or which is a landmark? Are the buildings arranged according to a plan?

Look at the ugly tower which is home to the richest Indian. And to think of all the money and effort that has gone into making it so spectacularly ugly.

A visit to our public hospitals is enough to convince anyone that the buildings themselves are sick. No thought is given to aesthetics or even purpose while constructing schools, government offices, courts and business complexes, all of which look alike.

Even our malls, multiplexes and airports lack imagination. Architecture has lost its enriching sense of purpose, all that matters is milking every square inch of Floor-Space Index (FSI). In the words of celebrated architect B V Doshi, Indian architecture today lacks context, content and a message.

Incidentally, he is from Ahmedabad and had worked with Kahn when he was designing the IIM-A in the late sixties. Doshi went on to design the IIM Bangalore, IIM Udaipur and NIFT Delhi as well as the '*Amdavad ni gufa*', an underground art gallery, and the Tagore hall in Ahmedabad.

India is at risk of losing its architectural identity, he feels because our design schools aren't teaching students to respect local heritage and traditions.

The doyen of architecture also says that many Indian architects are too concerned with aping the aesthetics and practices of other countries. For instance, the glass façade buildings which are good for trapping the scant sunlight in European countries but not in India which has a harsh sun. They may look bright and shiny but it takes a lot of electricity to cool them in tropical countries.

Ironically, this insensitivity to architecture was being shown in Ahmedabad. This is the city where the famous Le Corbusier, who designed Chandigarh, made four iconic buildings. This is the city which has the country's foremost architecture school, the Centre for Environment and Planning Technology (CEPT), and the premier design school, National Institute for Design.

Ahmedabad was also the place where Prince Khurram, to be Shah Jahan, who gave us the Taj Mahal, acquired a taste for architecture. As governor of Gujarat he was impressed by its architectural marvels such as the Jama Masjid in Ahmedabad, the magnificent structures of Champaner, the Adalaj step well and the Modhera sun temple.

Dull repetitive buildings are not only boring, they also have been clinically proven to induce stress. In some cities, citizens have voted to keep out such buildings. The Tour Montparnasse, a black skyscraper looming over the beautiful Paris cityscape is an example. Parisians hated it so much that the city was forced to enact a law forbidding any further skyscrapers higher than 36 metres.

On the other hand, it has been shown that people who work in well-designed spaces take less sick leave, are more focused, and generally contribute more to their company.

It may take us ages to rectify our blunders in concrete but a simple paintbrush can liven up things on the street as the group St+art India has shown. The non-profit group engages the public through huge, eye-catching murals painted on street corners, intersections or apartment buildings. It has created the country's first art district in Delhi's Lodhi Colony.

Coming back to Mumbai, you might be surprised to learn that it has the world's second-largest concentration of Art Deco buildings, characterized by streamlined forms and geometric motifs inspired by new technologies — ocean liners, airplanes, automobiles, etc.

It has more than 200 such structures including Eros Cinema, New India Assurance Building, Empress Court and the buildings lining Marine Drive. These are now part of a World Heritage site and hence have escaped redevelopment.

Redevelopment coupled with philistinism have led to the recent demolition and removal of the iconic Hall of Nations in Delhi's Pragati Maidan which ranked in the top 100 of the world's most significant buildings of the last century.

Bad architecture and design is not only robbing Indian cities of all character and charm, it is choking them at a time when the Covid pandemic has underlined the need to put people first and create livable cities.

Recite An Indian Love Poem to Your Valentine

The love poems of Bharatiya sanskriti must feature in Valentine's cards as well as in the curriculum.

Everyone must oppose the celebration of Valentine's Day in India because it is not in line with '*Bharatiya sanskriti*'. However, Indian culture is not what the so-called custodians of Indic culture claim it to be.

It is far richer, liberal and soulful than outfits such as the Sri Ram Sene or the Bajrang Dal can ever imagine, even on the subject of romantic love.

And most Indians – even those opposed to the '*desi*' Taliban – are as ignorant. Otherwise, Valentine's cards would have had Indian love poems rather than mushy English rhymes.

In fact, if the BJP wants to inculcate Indian culture in the new generation, it must include Indian love poems in the school and college syllabus. The tragedy is that they haven't read it themselves or they are as prudish as the Victorians, the Britishers whom they profess to hate.

Let's begin with the boy-meets-girl story in Hindu scriptures. Ram's first meeting with Sita was not at her '*swayamvar*', the competition where she chose her groom. The story goes like this: Sage Vishwamitra was being troubled by a female demon, Taraka, and asked for help from King Dashrath, who deputed his teenaged sons Ram and Lakshman. They escorted the sage to his forest ashram and slayed the demon. Some more adventures later, the duo ended up in Mithila where King Janak hosted the heroes. It is here in the gardens of the royal palace that Sita and Ram came face to face, fleetingly.

The rest is a much-repeated story. Now, Ram did not pluck a flower for Sita, nor did he recite a poem for her. Not a word was exchanged. As the cliché goes, it was love at first sight and the smitten princess ran back to the palace. Whether it was the power of love or a sage's divine blessing that gave Ram the superhuman strength to break Shiva's bow at the *'swayamvar'* is an open-ended question.

Now, let's look at ancient Indian love poems, which scholars say are not very different from global literature. Kalidas, the greatest Indian poet and playwright, born 2,000 years before Shakespeare, wrote these lines: 'Her hand upon her hip she placed, And swayed seductively her waist, With chin upon her shoulder pressed, She stretched herself to show her breast: With sapphire pupils burning bright within pearly orbs of white, Her eyes with eagerness did dance, And threw me a come-hither glance'. Scholars say that Indian love poems are often unhesitatingly sensual and describe women's 'ideal' physical form repeatedly, and in great detail.

This is also true of Bhartrhari, the sixth-century poet-philosopher to whom these lines are attributed: 'A man may tread the righteous path, Be master of his senses Retire in timidity Or cling to modest ways, Only until the arrow glances of amorous women fall on his heart'. The 12th-century poet Jayadeva's *'Geet Govinda'* describes the relationship between Krishna and Radhika and the *'gopikas'* in language that would make today's moral police see red.

It is full of erotic descriptions of love scenes between Radha and Krishna. For that matter, even the *Ramayana* and the *Mahabharata* do not display any squeamishness regarding sex. All these poems are in the *'Shringara ras'* tradition, which focuses on the emotional content of the sexual experience, with a rich vocabulary to express the myriad moods and emotions associated with it.

In the words of Richard Schiffman, an environmental journalist, author and poet, lovers stir the pot of their erotic attraction by seeing one another as embodiments of all their cravings and they spice it up by sharing secrets, making up affectionate names for one another, playing games, and giving inventive gifts. A reflection of this relationship between the divine couple, Radha and Krishna, is visible in Indian dance, music and theatre.

But why go back thousands of years? Take Ghalib, who said: '*Ishq par zor nahīñ hai, ye vo ātish 'ġhālib' ki lagā.e na lage aur bujhā.e na bane*' (Love is not in one's control, this is that fire roused, it cannot be willed to ignite, nor can it be doused).

Another of his '*shers*' made popular by Bollywood is: '*Ishq ne 'Ghālib' nikammā kar diyā varna ham bhī aadmī the kaam ke*' (Ghalib, a worthless person, this love has made of me otherwise a man of substance I once used to be) A third one attributed to him can only be confirmed by Ghalib fans: '*Labon pe honth rakh kar kaha tha uss zaalim ne, Kya shikwa, kya gila hai, ab bolte kyon nahin*'.

Take Ghalib's predecessor Meer Taqi Meer, who some claim is a better poet: '*Ibtedaae ishq hai, rota hai kya, aage aage dekhiye hotā hai kyā*' (It's only the beginning of love, why dost thou groan? O, wait and see what happens as you onward move).

The captivating part of Meer's poetry is the grief he expresses and these lines are typical of his work: '*Pattā, pattā buuTā, buuTā haal hamārā jaane hai, jaane na jaane gul hī na jaane baaġh to saarā jaane hai*' (Every leaf, every tree knows about my condition. Except for the flower, the entire garden knows of my longing for it).

Faiz Ahmed Faiz's '*Hum dekhenge*' was in the news during the Shaheen Bagh sit-in but he is known as a romantic poet: '*Aur kyā dekhne ko baaqī hai aap se dil lagāke dekh liyā*' (What else is worth seeing, now I have been a witness to your love).

Or sample this one: '*Dil nā-umiid to nahīñ nākām hī to hai, lambī hai ġham kī shaam magar shaam hī to hai*'. (My efforts [at love] stand thwarted, but my heart is optimistic. The evening of suffering goes on, but it too shall pass).

Talking of romantic ghazals, who can forget Farida Khanum's rendition of Fayyaz Hashmi's '*Aaj jaane ki zid na karo*' or Ghulam Ali's rendition of Maulana Hasrat Mohani's '*Chupke, chupke raat, din aansoo bahana yaad hai*'. All of them are Pakistanis but art transcends borders.

Lata Mangeshkar, who passed away last week, was just as popular in Pakistan. One can list any number of her immortal melodies: *'Lag ja gale ke phir ye haseen raat ho ke na ho, shayad is janam mein phir mulaqat ho ke ne ho;* 'Yeh kahaan aa gaye hum'; 'Aaja piya tohe pyaar doon'.

It is the exuberance of youth which has led to a Rose Day, Propose Day, Chocolate Day and Teddy Day in the run-up to Valentine's Day. They might as well include a Poetry Day and pen something from the heart.

Richie Rich and the Philanthropy Itch

Our capitalists take from the poor and take till it hurts.

As we head into Diwali, let us spread happiness by lighting up the lives of the less fortunate. But first, let's examine our attitude to caring and sharing: Do affluent Indians do their bit for the underprivileged? Are the rich into charity? Do our business tycoons give back to society? Finally, is philanthropy alien to our culture?

What better time to test these assumptions than the *annus horribilis* we are living through. The *'daan veer'* of these times is no Tata or Birla but a minor Bollywood star named Sonu Sood who bused migrant workers to their villages when the *'sarkar'* as well as the *'sahukars'* were playing blind, deaf and dumb.

Since Sonu Sood can't do everything, our Covid warriors are waiting for Christmas. That is when the doctors, nurses and ward boys who are still alive hope to get their salary arrears, not from the white-bearded man in a high office but from the one on a reindeer sleigh. That is the magic moment when the next-of-kin of those who have died on the Covid front will get the promised *'pravachan'*, sorry, *'parishramik'* (compensation).

Misery doesn't move us. The last *'sethia'* from the subcontinent to be perturbed by human suffering was Siddartha. Wonder if he ever came across something as stark as the sight of hundreds of poor cancer patients and their families living on the pavement outside Tata Memorial hospital at Parel in Mumbai. And this is the *El Dorado* of India!

Before we discuss philanthropy, let us look at the people who have the moolah for it; the handful of industrialists who hold most of India's wealth. However, it took a French economist, Thomas Piketty, to tell us of the extent of the inequity; the top one per cent of Indian earners have captured 22 per cent of its total income.

Our capitalists are not known to be considerate to their workers, much less in the lockdown. If you don't care for your employees, how can you be altruistic where society is concerned?

Of the several instances of shameful conduct by corporates, there is one about which I wrote as a journalist. A big financial institution was misusing its status as a sponsor to dictate terms to the Tata Institute of Social Sciences. It was hiring the institute's final-year students for their Corporate Social Responsibility (CSR) department but did not want the visually challenged.

CSR is a statutory '*daan*' which requires corporates to spend two per cent of their profits on eradicating hunger and poverty, promoting education and gender equality, promoting health care etc. However, it has not lived up to its promise.

One of the reasons is that the least developed states do not get the largest chunk of CSR funds. According to the Centre for Asian Philanthropy and Society (CAPS), Maharashtra got 15% of the pooled funds last year whereas Bihar got just 0.7%. There's inequity in charity too.

If you forget forced philanthropy, our capitalists take from the poor and take till it hurts; what are all our bank scams about? We may quote from the Gita about '*saattvika daan*', the purest form of donation, which is given to someone who can't return the favour and given in the right place and time but our *mool mantra* is '*Ram naam japna, paraya maal apna*'.

When natural disasters strike, corporates generally raise relief funds from their employees by unilaterally deducting a day's salary. Often, this money is invested and the principal, or part of it, is utilised much later.

It is not only the rich who rob. Our babus have a hoary tradition of gobbling up funds meant for the poor, they even eat from the mid-day meal schemes for poor kids. As for siphoning funds meant for drought relief, one only has to read P Sainath's book, *'Everyone loves a good drought'*. Surprisingly, rural development gets just 11% of CSR funds and figures way behind areas such as education (38%) and health (25%).

Here, a distinction must be made between charity and philanthropy. While the former is feeding someone fish, the latter is teaching him to fish. Indians are better at charity and they are just learning about philanthropy, as the dismal results of the CSR experiment show.

The concept of philanthropy in India (*'daan', 'dharma'*) is tied up with religion. We give to God who does not need money. We construct temples instead of hospitals, we pour milk on idols instead of feeding it to the mendicant outside. We bribe our way to a *'darshan'*, we even offer a bribe to the Lord to grant our wishes. We have a transactional relationship with God and the only thing we truly worship is wealth.

No wonder temples were complaining of dwindling funds during the lockdown. Except for *gurudwaras*, no one is feeding the needy during the pandemic. This is not to say that the offerings of devotees are not occasionally used for projects such as the free heart hospital at Puttaparthi in AP.

There's this case of a Konkan village which is deserted because of lack of water. Its inhabitants who work in Mumbai rejected a plan to recharge its underground streams because it cost Rs 18 lakh but had no compunctions in raising Rs 50 lakhs to renovate the village temple.

Indians also have the mentality of hoarding for the next seven generations. This is what Wipro's Azim Premji, one of our true philanthropists, was hinting at when he observed that a majority of wealthy Indians feel they must leave their entire money as an inheritance to their children. Truly, for us, charity begins at home.

That is why there are no Warren Buffets in India. The most charitable billionaire in America, outranking even Bill Gates, Buffet has given away $46 billion since 2000, about 71% of his fortune. In fact, when one looks at global business leaders, one associates philanthropy with entrepreneurial wealth whether it is Bill Gates, Elon Musk, Jack Ma or Mark Zuckerberg.

The legendary parsimony of Indians has given birth to several jokes, one of which goes like this: An Indian in the Gulf comes across a sheikh injured in a car crash and saves his life by rushing him to the hospital and donating blood to him. The grateful sheikh gifts him a Mercedes Benz. A year later, the same Indian saves his life in the same manner but this time he gets just a box of sweets. The sheikh explains to the perplexed Indian that now he too has Indian blood coursing through his veins!

Some say that this stinginess of Indians is not a byproduct of our culture but the malaise of the post-liberalization economic value system of loot-and-scoot. Another argument is that several of the Indian rich still think of themselves as middle class because they have made the transition in one generation. Piketty has also pointed out that the inequity in India rose sharply after liberalization in the '90s.

Of late though, a concerted effort is being made by people such as Azim Premji and Kiran Mazumdar-Shaw to promote the idea of philanthropy. Eleven Indian and Indian origin families such as Dr Romesh and Kathleen Wadhwani and Nandan and Rohini Nilekani, have joined the Giving Pledge, a commitment made by billionaires globally to donate the bulk of their wealth to philanthropic causes.

The middle class as usual contributes to spreading Diwali cheer in many ways; visiting an orphanage, an old-age home, contributing to the toy bank, volunteering for causes through websites such as *ivolunteer.in* or *karmayog. org*, pledging their organs after death or simply reaching out to the homeless in their localities.

Why Our Killer Serials Are About Serial Killers

Movies on multiple murders are the adult equivalent of monster movies for children.

I watch Nat Geo to Netflix to NDTV but my binge-watching in the times of Corona is essentially about serial killers; *Asur, Breathe, Mrs Serial Killer, Water bottle, Damaged...* After a point, I started wondering if there was something wrong with me or whether my morbid fascination with multiple murder had something to do with my days as a crime reporter.

But after comparing notes with fellow couch potatoes I was relieved to know that this addiction is no deviant behaviour, quite a few are hooked. In fact, I got some recommendations; *Dexter, The Alienist, Mr Mercedes, Making a Murderer, The Fall, The Following, Hannibal, The Ted Bundy tapes...*

So, why is it that so many of our killer serials are about serial killers? Why are we drawn to the stories of men and women who abduct, torture, rape, kill, engage in necrophilia and occasionally even eat another human being? Are they the adult equivalent of monster movies for children?

Well, for one, they are far more gripping than the other stuff on the menu; soppy soap operas, silly sitcoms or even the crafted reality shows. Seriously, can the *saas-bahu* serials or the talent competitions ever give you an adrenaline rush?

But before we delve into the mind of a couch-potato killer, let's trace the progression of the genre in India. First, it was the detective shows, *Karamchand* to *Byomkesh Bakshi* to *CID*, then came the true-life cases as in *Crime Patrol* and *Savdhaan India*, and now it has taken a quantum leap in web series where the spotlight is on the criminal rather than on the crime-buster.

The title role in *Asur* is that of a man with a troubled childhood who uses myth and mysticism to delude himself into believing that he is on a divine mission to rid the earth of those threatening social justice. The appeal of such serials goes beyond the audience, luring stars such as Arshad Warsi, R Madhavan and Abhishek Bachchan. Even the prim-and-proper Tata Sky uses Ashutosh Rana as a serial killer in its promo for their pulp fiction, *Adbhut Kahaniyan*.

In India though the serial killer genre is in its infancy, basically it's at the psychobabble stage. Hindi serials as well as films are about fictional characters except for a couple of movies loosely based on Raman Raghav, the schizophrenic who terrorized Mumbai during the sixties and the 'stoneman', who like Jack the Ripper, is still a mystery with the murders of nine pavement dwellers in Mumbai in 1989 attributed to him.

In my book, Charles Sobhraj, Cyanide Mohan and even Rajendra Jakkal and his accomplices in Pune's Joshi-Abhyankar murders don't classify as serial killers; they don't have that touch of insanity and the randomness in their choice of victims. The closest we have come to a classic serial killer in recent times are Surinder Koli of Nithari and Auto Shankar of Chennai.

The land of serial killers is America and their lore is part of popular culture there since the mid-seventies. In fact, they are transformed into larger-than-life celebrity monsters. It's a win-win formula; the TV channels get their TRPs while the public gets a safe conduit for its primal feelings: fear, lust and anger.

One such killer, David Berkowitz, fascinated me as a schoolboy. He prowled the streets of New York at night with a. 44 revolver and then sent postcards to the police gloating about his hits as The Son of Sam. Only now in the Netflix series, *Mindhunter*, currently our family-viewing at dinner, did I get to know the man and his motives. I have binge-watched it to the point where the FBI, having profiled a serial killer after several interviews with the jailed ones, is about to crack the murders of 20 black kids in Atlanta.

Analysing the appeal of the genre, script-writers, shrinks and criminologists all agree that the stories are unique and compelling; people want to know why seemingly normal human beings can be so perverse and brutal.

Making the 'art imitates life' argument, Bollywood script-writer Anjum Rajabali says, "Given the times we are living in, our fascination with the dark side of human nature is increasing". Serial killers, he adds, represent the darkest shade of the showbiz spectrum that begins with clean thrillers and progresses to private sleuths, cops, mafia dons, lone wolfs.

Budding media professional Harsh Mahatme saw the entire first season of *Fargo*, now in its fourth season, at a stretch. Engineering student Arhan Choudhury devoured three episodes at a time of *Mindhunter*, now in its third season. Even the aged mother of a friend confessed to watching *13 Commandments* in which the killer reverts to the 10 commandments to awaken the collective conscience and *Lincoln Rhyme* in which the killer plays a game of cat and mouse with two cops.

Indeed, both Harsh and Arhan say they were drawn to such serials by the psyche of the serial killers. Entrepreneur Thomas Abraham says he was captivated by 'the sense of menace' in *True Detectives*, season-1, and the naturally flawed characters in it, 'each offering a deeper meaning'.

Asked why viewers prefer serial killers over samaritans, psychiatrist Dayal Mirchandani attributes it to our survivalist mindset: "We have developed a negative bias to protect ourselves, we are looking out for danger all the time."

Criminologist Scott Bonn says in his blog that women are particularly fascinated by such killers because they have a greater fear of becoming the victim of a motivation-less crime. Another draw, he says, is that the senseless crimes are puzzling for women who are typically better at understanding the motivations, emotions, and actions of other people.

The jury is still out on the popularity of serial killer shows but one thing is certain, the catharsis guarantees you a good night's sleep.

✳ ✳ ✳

About the Author

Anil Kumar Singh has been a mainstream English journalist for four decades during which he was the Metro Editor of the flagship Mumbai edition of *The Times of India* for four years. He has chronicled Bombay, which has been his home, till it became Mumbai through the city's tryst with post-Babri riots, the ensuing serial blasts, the Mohalla Committees which restored trust in the police force, the underworld hit job on textile magnate Sunit Khatau, the deluge of July 26, 2005, the 2006 blasts in local trains, mills turning into malls, Mumbai's effusive welcome to Dhoni and his World Cup winning team, the 2008 terrorist attack on Mumbai, the game of musical chairs in Maharashtra…

Many events he covered from the ground have since become the subjects of OTT serials; the killing of crime reporter Jey Dey and the wrongful arrest of his colleague Jigna Vora for it, the murky world of encounter specialists in the police, the Telgi stamp paper scam and the Sheena Bora murder case.

Singh has been a sub-editor on the news desk as well as a reporter. After his active years, he's an independent journalist and journalism teacher. When not writing or teaching, he's either travelling or gardening.

***

www.ingramcontent.com/pod-product-compliance
Lightning Source LLC
Chambersburg PA
CBHW031552150726
47990CB00001B/313